Janet Stear

William Collins' dream of knowledge for all began with the publication of his first book in 1819. A self-educated mill worker, he not only enriched millions of lives, but also founded a flourishing publishing house. Today, staying true to this spirit, Collins books are packed with inspiration, innovation and practical expertise. They place you at the centre of a world of possibility and give you exactly what you need to explore it.

Collins. Freedom to teach

Published by Collins
An imprint of HarperCollins*Publishers*
77 – 85 Fulham Palace Road
Hammersmith
London
W6 8JB

Browse the complete Collins catalogue at
www.collinseducation.com

© HarperCollins*Publishers* Limited 2013

10 9 8 7 6 5 4 3 2 1

ISBN-13 978 0 00 752198 2

Janet Stearns asserts her moral right to be identified as the author of this work.

British Library Cataloguing in Publication Data
A Catalogue record for this publication is available from the British Library

Commissioned by Catharine Steers
Project managed by Sue Chapple
Production by Rebecca Evans

Typeset by Jouve India Private Limited
Edited by Philippa Boxer
Proof read by Pat Dunn
Indexed by Jane Coulter
Photo research by Shelley Noronha
Concept design by Angela English
Cover design by Angela English

Printed and bound in China

Acknowledgements
The publishers wish to thank the following for permission to reproduce photographs. Every effort has been made to trace copyright holders and to obtain their permission for the use of copyright material. The publishers will gladly receive any information enabling them to rectify any error or omission at the first opportunity.

Cover & p 1 Akindo/iStockphoto; p 3 Sergey Novikov/Shutterstock.com; p 5 Gold Stock Images/Shutterstock.com; p 7 Andy Dean Photography/Shutterstock.com; p 10 Dennis Kuvaev/Shutterstock.com; pp 14, 19, 27, 34, 37, 46, 50, 61, 74, 77, 92, 99, 102, 105, 132, 138, 153, 160, 163, 188 Shutterstock.com; p 16 Craig Dingle/Istockphoto.com; p 23 Alexey Losevich/Shutterstock.com; p 31 D.Hurst/Alamy; p 40 Vanessa Davies/Getty Images; p 42 Robert Kneschke/Shutterstock.com; p 47 Chepko Danil Vitalevich/Shutterstock.com; p 53 Statutory Framework 2012/Crown Copyright; p 56 Steve Allen/Getty Images; p 58 Science Photo Library/Alamy; p 65 Peter H Noyce/Alamy; p 70 EYFS document 2012/Crown Copyright; p 80 Daniel Dupuis/Shutterstock.com; p 84 John Wollwerth/Shutterstock.com; p 87 Sally & Richard Greenhill/Alamy; p 89 Hywit Dimyadi/Shutterstock.com; p 96 ImagesBazaar/Getty Images; p 109 CandyBox Images/Alamy; p 114 Warren Goldswain/Shutterstock.com; p 116 Jo Unruh/Getty Images; p 121 Elena Schweitzer/Shutterstock.com; p 122 iStockphoto.com; p 127 Sergey Novikov/Shutterstock.com; p 130 Neo Edmund/Shutterstock.com; p 147 Jaimie Duplass/Shutterstock.com; p 150 Omer N Raja/Shutterstock.com; p 156 NICCY/image provided by Northern Ireland Commissioner for Children and Young People; p 167 Robert Kneschke/Shutterstock.com; p 169 Jaren Jai Wicklund/Shutterstock.com; p 173 Oksana Kuzmina/Shutterstock.com; p 176 Everett Collection Historical/Alamy; p 179 Oksana Kuzmina/Shutterstock.com; p 182 Fotosearch/Getty Images; p 187 Alena Ozerova/Shutterstock.com; p 190 Suzanne Tucker/Shutterstock.com

Contents

Active learning

Children learn actively and make sense of their world by thinking and investigating rather than passively through instruction. They adjust their knowledge as they encounter different situations and construct their ideas as they make sense of their experiences. In this way, children build their own meanings by applying what they know. Active learning enables children to build a framework for thinking and learning through interacting with their environment.

The importance of active learning

Children's direct experiences and interactions are central to their learning. When children are actively involved in learning, they are creating the mental structures that help them to develop their thinking (see *Creative, critical thinking*). Young children explore their world through movement and through problem-solving, using all their senses to find out what they can do.

Children build understanding and ideas from these early sensory experiences as they make new discoveries. This is particularly important for children with special needs or children who are learning English as an additional language (see *Communication*).

Supporting active learning

Early years practitioners can best support active learning by promoting children's involvement and setting them problems to solve. Play activities that are based on real life experiences, for example having a new baby in the family, help children to make connections between their play behaviour and their developing understanding. Activities that build on what children already know help to develop their self-esteem, confidence and ability to learn (see *Learning through play*).

Supporting active learning also involves creating the right conditions for children's learning. Early learning is interactive, messy, energetic and often physical. Practitioners should make full use of the outdoors in supporting children's active learning.

Decision-making is a very important part of active learning. Practitioners should encourage children to make decisions in their play by providing a wide variety of materials, which are accessible for all children, and setting them problems to solve.

Regular observation enables practitioners to monitor how children engage in different activities. This information can be used to develop children's play and active learning.

Case in point

Alex, aged four years, attends Little Stars Nursery and frequently chooses to play in the construction area outdoors. Alex enjoys playing with the large wooden blocks and creates intricate structures with towers and ramps.

Casey is Alex's key person. She has been observing and monitoring his play and thinking about supporting his active learning.

One day, Casey provides a selection of different wheeled vehicles and invites Alex to roll the vehicles down a wooden ramp he has created. She encourages him to compare the vehicles by setting him problems to work out actively for himself.

Casey also provides building tools and equipment in the sand play area outside to broaden the context of Alex's construction play.
In this way, Casey is providing opportunities to support Alex's active learning and promoting the development of his knowledge and understanding.

Summary

Children's interactions with their environment lead to mental processes through which they construct their ideas. Active learning enables children to adjust and structure their knowledge and build their own meanings by applying, revising and reapplying what they know. This helps children to become creative, critical thinkers and supports their learning and development.

Antenatal provision

Antenatal provision refers to the care a woman receives during her pregnancy before the birth of the baby. It includes regular check-ups, routine examinations and specialised tests as well as education, guidance and preparation for the birth. The aim of antenatal provision is to monitor the growth of the baby and the health of the mother in order to support a successful pregnancy, labour and delivery.

Health in pregnancy

The health of the mother has a direct impact on the developing embryo. Pregnant women need to eat healthily and avoid potentially damaging substances such as alcohol and other drugs, as this can cause developmental problems for the baby. Research has shown that smoking cigarettes in pregnancy can increase the chance of low birth weight and cot death (see *Cot death*), and that stress can be harmful to the unborn baby. Pregnant women should not take any medication unless it has been prescribed by a doctor.

Infectious diseases like German measles (rubella) can cause damage to the developing embryo such as deafness, blindness and heart defects. Pregnant women should avoid being in contact with anyone who has an infectious illness, particularly during the first trimester of their pregnancy (see *Development in-utero*).

Nutrition in pregnancy

A pregnant woman's diet should be well balanced and include all the main nutrients, particularly protein, iron and calcium. The developing embryo takes all the nutrients it requires for its own growth and this can leave the mother's own supply low. She should eat plenty of fresh fruit and vegetables, milk, fish, meat or soya protein. Folic acid is an important supplement which is usually prescribed by the doctor during pregnancy as it can help prevent birth defects.

Some foods contain bacteria that can be harmful to the developing embryo and should be avoided by the pregnant woman. These include soft cheeses (such as Brie) and raw eggs.

Antenatal care

It is important for women to have regular check-ups throughout their pregnancy. Ideally this should begin during the first 12 weeks and will usually be carried out by a midwife.

This routine care will include both blood and urine tests and will monitor the woman's weight gain and blood pressure. High blood pressure can be a sign of pre-eclampsia, which is a very dangerous condition for both mother and baby.

Some tests in pregnancy are not carried out routinely but may be offered for specific reasons. For example, an amniocentesis may be performed to test for genetic conditions such as Down's syndrome (see *Atypical development*).

Antenatal care will also involve preparation for the birth of the baby, including information about pain relief in labour.

Summary

Antenatal provision is extremely important for the health and wellbeing of the mother and baby. Regular check-ups help to monitor the development of the baby and minimise any potential risk factors. This helps to establish a healthy start in life and improve outcomes for both the mother and baby.

Reference

NHS Choices http://www.nhs.uk/

Attachment

The term 'attachment' was first defined by John Bowlby in the 1950s as the strong, emotional relationship or bond between children and their main carers. He highlighted how important this connection is for children's emotional security and developing sense of self. By building on this firm foundation, most young children are able to develop confidence, become more independent and learn to get along with others.

Developing attachment relationships

The development of a strong attachment relationship is particularly important in the first year of life. It is established initially between the primary carer and baby through nurturing behaviour, the provision of a consistent, caring routine and by responding sensitively to the baby's needs. Eye contact, smiling, loving communication and affectionate, physical touch can all positively influence the development of attachment relationships between children and their main carers.

Research on infant brain growth has shown that this kind of nurturing behaviour results in the production of the chemical dopamine in the brain. Dopamine is an important neuro-transmitter (chemical messenger) associated with feelings of enjoyment and motivation.

Babies who are deprived of nurturing experience a negative impact on their emotional development and fail to thrive. Many factors can interfere with the development of strong attachment relationships, including prematurity, post-natal depression, abuse, stress, and indeed anything that might cause the primary carer to be unresponsive to the infant.

Impact on children's development

A strong attachment relationship provides children with a 'secure base' from which they can explore the world with confidence and it also creates a firm foundation for all other areas of development:

➤ Physically, children are more confident, keen to explore and take risks.

➤ Cognitively, children are more self-assured, with an improved disposition to learn.

➤ Socially, children are more trusting and self-confident in making relationships with others.

➤ Emotionally, children are secure and independent, with well-developed self-esteem.

Children who feel secure also develop greater resilience, which helps them to deal with stress (see *Resilience*). Children who do not develop secure attachment relationships often have emotional and behavioural problems and can have difficulty in developing relationships with others.

Influence on early years practice

Attachment theory underpins many aspects of current early years practice, including the key person approach, settling-in procedures and helping children to deal with transitions. A key person in an early years setting will develop a strong attachment relationship with each of the children in his or her care (see *Key person*), which will help the children to settle in when they start at an early years setting. Children who feel secure will have a sense of belonging, which will help them to manage difficult times like separating from their parent and dealing with transitions (see *Transitions*).

Research has shown that young children can make secure attachments with a number of different carers without any harmful effects on their emotional development.

Summary

A strong attachment relationship is essential for children's holistic development. It is particularly important for healthy emotional development and helps children to build resilience and develop self-esteem. In early years settings, it is important for young children to develop an attachment relationship with a key person and this forms a vital foundation for their welfare and wellbeing.

References

BOWLBY, J. (2005) *A Secure Base*. London: Routledge.

Department for Education (2012) *Statutory Framework for the Early Years Foundation Stage*. http://www.education.gov.uk

ELFER, P., GOLDSCHMIED, E. & SELLECK, D. (2011) *Key Persons in the Early Years: Building Relationships for Quality Provision in Early Years Settings and Primary Schools*. London: Routledge.

Atypical development

Atypical development is development that deviates from the expected or usual pattern. There are many reasons why children's development may be atypical, including a result of global delay (all areas of development), specific delay (for example, in speech and language) or development which exceeds the expected pattern (for example, gifted and talented).

Factors affecting children's development

All children develop in their own unique way, but if development is not following the expected pattern, it is important to recognise this and to implement early intervention in order to maximise the child's potential.

There are many different factors that can affect children's development, both positively and negatively. Some of these factors are biological, such as health or disability, and some are due to external factors, such as poverty and stress.

The pre-natal period is an extremely important stage in child development (see *Development in-utero*), and factors such as smoking cigarettes or poor nutrition in pregnancy can have a significant impact on children's development. Premature babies (born before the 37th week of pregnancy) often take extra time to reach developmental milestones, such as sitting up or learning to walk (see *Prematurity*).

Disability, long-term medical conditions and short-term illnesses can all impact on children's development. Children who are born with Down's syndrome can experience different degrees of developmental delay, and learning difficulties affecting speech and language development, body coordination and cognitive abilities.

Family values, parenting style and cultural factors also affect children's development. Some parents provide support for their children's early education with play and activities at home. In some cultures, children are pressured to achieve academically from a very young age. Parental divorce and other factors within the family, such as drug or alcohol abuse, can result in children feeling insecure, with subsequent effects on their all-round development.

Impact of atypical development

Global delay can affect all areas of children's development, including physical, cognitive, communication, social and emotional. Developmental delay in a specific area can also have an impact on children's all-round development. For example, if a child's language skills are not developing, they will have difficulty in communicating or making themselves understood. This will influence both their social and emotional development, as it will be difficult for them to express themselves and make friendships. If this is not addressed, the child will start to lose confidence and may develop a negative attitude and challenging behaviour.

Children whose development exceeds the expected pattern can also experience difficulties, including frustration or boredom due to under-stimulation and difficulties in making friendships or interacting with peers.

Recognising atypical development

It is important to be able to recognise atypical development at an early stage to provide support for the child and their family. Early years practitioners can do this through regular observations and routine monitoring of children's development and by ongoing communication with parents. Recognition of atypical development is often the starting point for early intervention. This may involve the child being assessed by a number of different professionals to determine the best way to provide help and support (see *Early intervention*). Delays in development can be rectified quickly if they are identified early.

It is always important to listen carefully to the parents and to take full account of the family history. Many cases of atypical development follow familial patterns, for example being a 'late talker'.

Case in point

Andrew is four years old and has Down's syndrome. He attends Little Acorns Nursery every morning. His key person, Amy, makes regular observations of Andrew's developmental progress and she has noticed that he can pedal a tricycle and catch a large ball, although he has difficulty with some fine motor skills, such as using scissors. He likes familiar routines and quickly becomes upset if things change suddenly. Andrew can communicate using some spoken language and understands simple instructions. Amy works with Andrew's speech and language therapist and has learned some Makaton signs to help her communicate with Andrew.

Amy knows that Andrew's development will not follow the expected pattern and she works closely with his parents to plan activities that are appropriate to Andrew's stage of development and interests rather than his chronological age.

Summary

All children develop in their own way and at their own rate. However, not all children follow the expected pattern and this can be caused by several different factors. Monitoring children's development is very important in supporting their wellbeing and measuring their progress. Early years practitioners need to be able to recognise atypical development and respond appropriately.

Reference

STEARNS, J., SCHMIEDER, C. & YOUNG, K. (2013) *BTEC National Children's Play, Learning and Development.* London: HarperCollins Publishers.

Basic needs of children

Children have certain basic needs that have to be met in order for them to grow and thrive. These include food, sleep, safety, stimulation, love and belonging. Early years practitioners must have a thorough understanding of all children's needs and be able to meet the individual needs of children in different situations.

Maslow's hierarchy of needs

Abraham Maslow (1908–1970) was an American psychologist who developed the 'hierarchy of needs'. He represented this as a pyramid, with the basic needs at the bottom and the goal of 'self-actualisation' at the top. According to Maslow, children can only reach their full potential (or 'self-actualisation') if their basic needs are satisfied first.

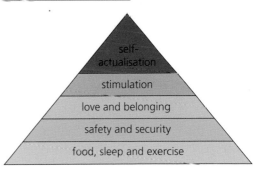

self-actualisation

stimulation

love and belonging

safety and security

food, sleep and exercise

Each layer of the pyramid, from the bottom up, has to be satisfied before the next can be fully achieved.

The need for food

A healthy, balanced diet is essential for children's growth and development (see *Healthy eating*). Early years practitioners should make sure that children have access to healthy, nutritious food and fresh drinking water.

The need for sleep

Children need regular rest and sleep to help them develop. Research has shown that sleep plays an important role in allowing the body to grow and children who do not get enough sleep often become irritable and upset. Babies need at least 12 hours of sleep every night and most three-year-olds will still need a rest or nap during the day.

Practitioners need to make sure that daily routines allow for periods of rest and sleep.

The need for exercise

Exercise is important for children's physical development. It provides opportunities to practise physical skills, encourages confidence and helps to reduce the risk of childhood obesity. Exercise helps to build strong muscles, improves body coordination and helps to establish lifelong attitudes towards health and fitness. Practitioners should provide opportunities for children to exercise daily, both indoors and outside of the setting.

The need for safety

Children need to feel safe, both physically and emotionally. It helps them feel secure and confident, enables them to express themselves and supports their inclination to learn. Practitioners need to create a safe environment and support children to feel secure in the setting.

The need for love and belonging

All children need to feel loved. It makes them feel valued, builds self-esteem and helps them feel special. A sense of belonging makes children feel included and appreciated. Early years practitioners need to develop strong attachment relationships with children and create a nurturing environment in the setting (see *Key person*).

The need for stimulation

Children learn through exploring and investigating. Practitioners need to provide a range of interesting activities to stimulate curiosity and encourage children's learning and development.

Case in point

Sophia is three years old and attends Treetops Nursery. She had a good night's sleep and ate breakfast before leaving for nursery. Her mother dropped her off at nursery on time with her teddy bear and gave her a hug before she left. Sophia's key person who met her on arrival had prepared one of Sophia's favourite games.

Rhianna is also three years old and attends Treetops Nursery. She has been awake for half the night because her baby brother was crying. Her mother overslept, so there was no time for breakfast. She forgot Rhianna's teddy bear and left without saying goodbye.

Sophia's basic needs for food, sleep, safety, security, love and belonging and stimulation have all been met. She is therefore starting her day at Treetops Nursery well prepared to achieve her full potential in learning and development.

In contrast, Rhianna's basic needs have not been met. She is starting her day at Treetops Nursery feeling tired, hungry, unloved and insecure. It is likely that she will spend her day feeling anxious and worried, rather than making the most of the stimulation on offer in the setting.

Summary

Maslow's theory states the importance of meeting children's basic needs in order for them to develop and learn. Early years practitioners need to be mindful of all children's individual needs so that they can thrive and achieve their full potential.

Reference

MASLOW, A. (2011) *Toward a Psychology of Being*. New York USA: Martino Fine Books.

Bullying

Bullying is the use of aggression (physical, verbal or non-verbal attacks) to exert power over someone else. It is extremely damaging to young children. Bullying is not always easy to describe, but it includes intimidation, harassment and discrimination with the intention of hurting another person.

Types of bullying

The charity Kidscape estimates that 1 in 12 children are so badly bullied that it affects their education, relationships and even their prospects for jobs in later life (Kidscape, 2012).

Bullying can take many different forms and frequently involves a combination of methods, including:

➤ Physical: pushing, kicking, hitting and other forms of violence or threats

➤ Verbal: name-calling, insults, sarcasm, spreading rumours or persistent teasing

➤ Emotional: humiliation, exclusion, tormenting and ridicule

➤ Cyber bullying: the use of technology, including mobile phones, the internet and social networking sites, to deliberately insult or ridicule someone.

Bullying behaviour can focus on a variety of characteristics, but with young children it commonly focuses on race, obesity and children with physical disabilities or special educational needs. The effects of persistent bullying can result in low self-esteem, depression, isolation and poor academic achievement (see *Challenging behaviour*).

Responding to concerns about bullying

Any incidence of bullying behaviour or threats of bullying must be reported and fully investigated without delay. Dealing with bullying incidents can be distressing for everyone concerned, particularly the child being bullied. It is important to treat each situation seriously and remember that both the victim and the bully will need support.

➤ Children who are bullied feel frightened and upset and may find it difficult to tell anyone. They must be reassured that the bullying will be stopped and they will be supported.

➤ Children who are involved in bullying others need to understand that their behaviour is not acceptable, and they should be supported to develop more positive behaviour patterns.

➤ The families of both victims and bullies also need support. It can be stressful for parents to discover that their child has been involved in bullying, either as a victim or as a bully.

All schools are required by law to have an anti-bullying policy which should involve children as well as staff, parents and carers. It is not a legal requirement in early years settings but is considered good practice.

Preventing bullying

One of the best ways to address bullying is to help prevent it in the first place. In early years settings, children can become more aware of this process by:

➤ helping to create the rules about behaviour in the setting

➤ being involved in decision-making to develop independence and assertiveness

➤ drawing and displaying pictures about preventing bullying

➤ sharing books and stories about bullying

➤ using puppets or Persona dolls to explore bullying behaviour.

The charity Kidscape provides a wide variety of information about preventing bullying and supporting children to protect themselves, including staying safe online.

Case in point

Anna works as a teaching assistant at Highgate Primary School and she frequently supervises the children at break times, when they are playing outside. Marlena is a five-year-old girl who attends Highgate Primary School. She is tall for her age and very overweight. Anna has noticed that a small group of girls have started teasing Marlena about her size and calling her names such as 'Fatty'. These children exclude Marlena from their games and she is often left on her own at play times. Anna speaks to her supervisor about what she has seen and together they decide to plan some activities with the children to reinforce their rule about being kind to each other. They choose some books and stories about bullying to share with the children and plan some circle time activities using Persona dolls and puppets to support their message. Anna also prepares some information to share with the children's parents about the anti-bullying activities and policies in the setting.

Summary

Bullying comes in a variety of different forms. Everybody has the right to be treated with respect and no one deserves to be a victim of bullying. Children who bully need to learn different ways of behaving and those who are the victims of bullying behaviour need to be supported. Early years practitioners have a responsibility to be vigilant for signs of bullying and to respond promptly. Settings should have effective policies in place to prevent bullying.

Reference

Kidscape http://www.kidscape.org.uk

Career development

There are many ways in which it is possible to further a career in childcare. Working with children offers a wide range of employment opportunities and there are many different ways to gain relevant qualifications in childcare and early years. The government report *More Great Childcare* (DfE, 2013) suggests even more opportunities for career progression.

Types of employment

There is a wealth of employment opportunities for qualified early years practitioners, including working with babies or young children in nurseries, children's centres or pre-school playgroups, taking care of children in their own home as a nanny or becoming a registered childminder. Practitioners may also work as a teaching assistant in a school, with children who have special educational needs, or with children in hospital.

Further qualifications enable early years practitioners to take on leadership roles and become managers in a variety of childcare settings.

Training and qualifications

Working with children is a professional role and it is important to have the right training to gain the appropriate qualifications. Early years training is available through schools, colleges and private training organisations in addition to 'on the job' training through apprenticeship programmes.

The knowledge and skills gained through early years qualifications can help students progress towards many other professional training programmes, for example in teaching or children's social work.

The wide variety of qualifications in childcare and early years can sometimes seem confusing. Qualifications in childcare and early years vary from one job to another and the different levels lead to jobs with varying amounts of professional responsibility. Here is a general overview of the qualification levels in early years:

Entry level: provides an introduction to the basic skills required for working with children. It is not a qualification for employment in early years, but provides support for moving on to the next level.

Level 1: builds on the basic skills gained at entry level and provides further knowledge and skills for working with children. It is not a qualification for employment in early years, but provides support for progression.

Level 2: provides the knowledge and skills for employment with children in a supervised role, for example as an assistant in a nursery or a school. Level 2 qualifications usually require students to undertake some practical placement experience.

Level 3: provides more advanced knowledge and skills for employment with children in a supervisory role, for example as an early years practitioner in a nursery or children's centre. Level 3 qualifications require students to undertake some practical placement experience and include taking responsibility as well as exercising individual judgement.

Level 4 and Level 5: build on Level 3 qualifications and provide the skills and knowledge required for leadership roles, for example as a manager of a nursery or pre-school group. Level 4 and 5 qualifications include taking responsibility for planning and developing early years curricula.

Level 6: provides a degree-level qualification (for example, as an Early Years Professional or Graduate Early Years Teacher) and the skills to lead and improve practice within early years settings as well as to support and inspire other staff.

The future

Professor Cathy Nutbrown's 2012 review of early years qualifications made a number of recommendations for change. The Early Years Educator qualification will become the new Level 3 qualification from September 2014. There will be a high proportion of practical work experience in these courses and students must have at least a C grade in GCSE English and mathematics.

The new Early Years Teacher qualification was introduced in September 2013. This builds on the strengths of the Early Years Professional Status and Early Years Teachers will be specialists in early childhood development and also be trained to work with babies and young children.

Case in point

Becky works at Rainbows Nursery. After leaving school, she achieved her Level 2 Certificate in Child Care and Education and qualified with the Level 3 Diploma two years ago. She has just been promoted to Room Leader with the pre-school children. Becky would like to become a nursery manager and is planning to study part-time for the Level 5 Diploma in Leadership.

Rob has just achieved the Level 3 Certificate in Supporting Teaching and Learning in Schools. He is working as a special educational needs assistant in a primary school and plans to study for his Early Years Teacher qualification next year.

Summary

The early years sector offers an extensive range of training programmes, qualifications and opportunities for career development. Qualified early years practitioners can gain employment in a variety of jobs with children and in a range of different settings.

References

Council for Awards in Care, Health and Education (CACHE) http://www.cache.org.uk

Department for Education (2013) *More Great Childcare: Raising Quality and Giving Parents More Choice*. http://www.education.gov.uk

Challenging behaviour

'Challenging behaviour' is a term used to describe inappropriate or unacceptable behaviour in children. It conflicts with accepted values and beliefs. As well as the more widely seen examples, challenging behaviour includes specific behavioural problems, such as Attention Deficit Disorder (ADD), hyperactivity or self-harm.

Types of challenging behaviour

Challenging behaviour is frequently demonstrated through physical actions, speech or non-verbal behaviour. This includes: pushing, hitting or biting other children; throwing or breaking toys; and shouting at adults or other children, and using offensive language.

Triggers

Many factors can act as triggers for children's challenging behaviour in the short term, including tiredness, hunger, boredom or illness. These can make children withdrawn and uncooperative, and some children experiencing transitions may display signs of regression (see *Transitions*).

Some long-term factors, such as abuse and bullying, can have more serious consequences. Such factors can affect children's behaviour in a variety of ways, including causing a lack of confidence, developmental regression or inappropriate aggression. Bullying can also have a negative influence on children's behaviour (see *Bullying*).

Different cultural influences can affect children's behaviour, as well as social factors both within and outside of the family, including parenting style, family structure, educational experience and the wider community. Children's behaviour is also influenced by their age and stage of development as they mature and understand what is expected of them.

Some conditions have specific effects on children's behaviour, including Attention Deficit Hyperactivity Disorder (ADHD) and Autistic Spectrum Disorder (ASD).

Dealing with challenging behaviour

Children often act impulsively and have difficulty in expressing their feelings and controlling their behaviour, especially at certain ages. Early years practitioners need to have realistic expectations about children's behaviour, based on a sound understanding of their development. It is also important to provide ways for children to express themselves through creative activities, for example through play with puppets, painting or pounding clay.

Any strategy for dealing with challenging behaviour needs to be applied consistently and fairly by all the adults involved so that children understand what is expected of them.

Strategies for managing behaviour
Effective management of behaviour should start with praise and encouragement for pro-social behaviours and self-regulation. This should be accompanied by distraction, redirection, withdrawal of attention, and logical and natural consequences for challenging behaviour. Most children crave attention from adults and if this is denied, it tells them that their behaviour is not acceptable.

One strategy that uses this principle is often referred to as 'time out', in this case time out from adults' attention. Children are removed from the presence of the adult for a short period to have some time and space to calm down. This creates a non-rewarding environment for unacceptable behaviour. However, this is not recommended for the youngest of children.

Other strategies include the following:

➤ Regular observation of children in the setting can help practitioners to identify the trigger for children's challenging behaviour, and ongoing communication with parents will help practitioners to plan appropriate support.

➤ Some children may require medication in order to manage their challenging behaviour, for example children with ADHD.

➤ Behaviour management plans are often used in early years settings to help practitioners understand children's behaviour more fully and develop effective action plans.

Case in point

Malik is almost five years old and will be moving into the first year of primary school after the summer break. His parents have recently divorced and Malik is living with his mother and grandmother. At nursery school, Andrea has been Malik's key person for the last year and she has noticed some worrying changes in his behaviour. He has become uncooperative and aggressive and he frequently hits other children. He refuses to participate in group activities and screams loudly if Andrea tries to encourage him.

Andrea understands that Malik is dealing with stressful change in his life. She speaks with Malik's mother and they develop a behaviour plan for him. Andrea provides various play activities for Malik to express his feelings, including clay, painting and puppets. Andrea regularly spends some quiet time alone with Malik to provide positive attention and they share some books about starting school. She sets clear expectations for Malik's behaviour, which she reinforces consistently, and observes Malik's behaviour daily, providing regular updates for his mother.

Summary

Many factors can influence children's behaviour and early years practitioners need to have a sound understanding of child development in order to have realistic expectations about children's behaviour. This knowledge and understanding helps practitioners to implement appropriate strategies and support children's behaviour. Practitioners need to be consistent and positive in their approach and model appropriate behaviour through their own actions and conduct (see *Positive behaviour*).

Reference

STEARNS, J., SCHMIEDER, C. & YOUNG, K. (2013) *BTEC National Children's Play, Learning and Development.* London: HarperCollins Publishers.

Childhood illness

Illness usually occurs as a result of a disease or condition which leads to a deterioration in normal health. In most cases, childhood illness is temporary. However, it can sometimes be life-threatening. Illnesses such as chickenpox are infectious and some, such as asthma, often need long-term treatment.

Signs of illness

Young children often find it difficult to describe how they feel. They may say that they have 'tummy ache' when they actually feel upset, afraid or worried. Some of the common signs of illness in young children include:

➤ Change in behaviour (unusually quiet, not sleeping well, crying more than usual)

➤ Poor appetite

➤ No energy

➤ Constipation or diarrhoea

➤ Vomiting

➤ Skin rash

➤ Raised body temperature

➤ A cough, headache, stomach ache, earache or runny nose

➤ Not gaining weight.

In an early years setting, any child showing signs of illness should be isolated and their parents should be contacted immediately. The child's key person should stay with them and observe them closely.

Infectious illnesses

Infectious illnesses are caused by bacteria or viruses and are spread mainly in the air (droplet infection) or through direct contact with an infected person (see *Cross-infection*). Most infectious illnesses start with symptoms such as a bad cold, with a slight rise in body temperature, a sore throat and generally feeling unwell. Other illnesses, such as chickenpox, also produce specific symptoms including a rash. Children with infectious illnesses should always be seen by a doctor and should be isolated until they are no longer infectious.

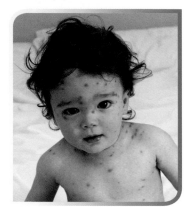

Meningitis

Meningitis is a serious infectious illness caused by either bacteria or a virus. It affects the meninges (the protective covering around the brain and spinal cord) and common symptoms are headache, neck stiffness and a high body temperature. It can also cause a blotchy skin rash, which does not fade under pressure, and this is usually a serious sign of the illness. Emergency action needs to be taken if meningitis is suspected as it can be life-threatening and the child may need to be admitted to hospital.

Non-infectious conditions

Some illnesses are not infectious, but require long-term treatment.

Asthma

Asthma is a chronic respiratory disorder characterised by wheezing, difficulty in breathing and coughing at night. It is usually triggered by an allergic reaction to materials such as pollen or animal fur. Many children with asthma can manage their symptoms with an inhaler. This helps to control the condition and prevent an asthma attack.

Diabetes

Type 1 diabetes is the most common type of diabetes that occurs in children. It is caused by the body's inability to produce enough insulin and a difficulty in regulating blood sugar levels. The management of type 1 diabetes usually involves monitoring the amount of sugar and carbohydrate in the child's diet and giving daily injections of insulin. Many children learn how to check their own blood sugar levels and to inject their own insulin from a very early age.

Care of a sick child

Being ill can be a frightening experience for young children and they need lots of attention and reassurance. Sick children often lose their appetite, so meals should be small, with plenty of water to drink. Their room should be warm and well ventilated, and their body temperature should be monitored regularly. Sick children have less energy and so enjoy quiet play activities, such as looking at picture books or having stories read to them.

It is very important to keep full records of any illness and to report to parents (see *Recording and reporting*).

When to call the doctor

When children are sick, their condition can improve very quickly but it can also worsen rapidly. It is important to know when to call the doctor or send for emergency medical help.

Medical help should always be called when a child has:

➤ a high temperature of 39°C or above

➤ breathing difficulties or becomes unconscious

➤ a convulsion or fit

➤ very severe or constant diarrhoea and/or vomiting

➤ a purple/red rash that does not fade under pressure.

Condition	Signs	Action to be taken in an early years setting
Food poisoning	Diarrhoea and vomiting	• Call the parents and seek medical advice.
Asthma	Difficulty in breathing	• Use the child's prescribed inhaler. • Call an ambulance if no improvement.
Diabetic (hypoglycaemic) coma	Sweating, dizziness, confusion, loss of consciousness	• Give the child something sweet such as chocolate or a sweet drink. • Call an ambulance if no improvement.
Meningitis	High temperature, severe headache, vomiting Purple/red rash that does not fade under pressure	• Call an ambulance immediately.
Severe allergic reaction	Swelling, rash, difficulty in breathing	• Use the child's prescribed auto-injector. • Call an ambulance.

Summary

It is important for early years practitioners to be able to recognise the signs of illness and to know what to do when children are sick. Children's symptoms can worsen very quickly and they should always be taken seriously and not ignored.

References

Asthma UK http://www.asthma.org.uk

Diabetes UK http://www.diabetes.org.uk

Children in care

Children are sometimes unable to live with their own family for a variety of reasons. Their parents might be unable to care for them, a parent may have a serious illness or they may have been neglected or abused by their parents. Children who are unable to live with their birth family are often referred to as 'looked-after children' and are usually taken care of by local authorities.

Foster care

Looked-after children can be placed in long- or short-term foster care, depending on their individual circumstances. This may happen for a variety of reasons, including abuse or neglect, family breakdown, parental illness, addiction or imprisonment.

Foster care involves placing a child with a family who will provide care and support on a temporary basis, and the child is treated as part of the family. However, a foster carer does not have parental rights and the local authority becomes the child's legal guardian.

Foster care gives the child the experience of living in a supportive family structure, but it can lead to problems for some children because of its temporary nature.

Residential care

Some looked-after children are placed in residential care homes. Residential care homes are institutional environments where children do not experience the same kind of emotional relationships as living in a foster family. Nevertheless, in some difficult situations, residential care does provide vulnerable children with a professional level of care and offers children a place of safety if they are removed from their family by a court order.

Children may be placed in residential care if they have experienced unsuccessful foster care placements or if they have extremely challenging behaviour. The local authority will usually act as the legal guardian for children in residential care.

Problems for children in care

Children who are taken into care often feel lonely and scared, and are emotionally distressed. They frequently suffer from attachment disorders and have difficulty developing trusting relationships. Many children in the care system are dealing with feelings of being rejected, abandoned and unloved. This can lead to challenging behaviour, relationship difficulties and problems in school (see *Challenging behaviour*).

Research by the NSPCC into the lives and experiences of children in care has shown that their educational attainments are poorer and they are more at risk of developing mental health problems (NSPCC, 2013).

Case in point

Carrie was only 17 when her son, Jamie, was born. She was abandoned by Jamie's father and lived with her mother, who struggled with depression. Carrie worked hard to care for Jamie, but when he was two years old, Carrie's mother was admitted into hospital for treatment for depression. Jamie was a demanding toddler and Carrie found it hard to manage his behaviour on her own. Carrie's new boyfriend, Wesley, moved in with her. He was an alcoholic and a drug addict. The standard of Jamie's care gradually deteriorated until social services were alerted and Jamie was taken into care.

Jamie was cared for in a foster family for eight months. During that time, Carrie had the support of a social worker and worked hard to get her life back on track. She left Wesley, started a new relationship and moved into different accommodation.

Carrie sees Jamie regularly and is now working towards getting him back on a permanent basis with the support of her social worker.

Summary

Local authorities throughout the UK provide residential care homes for looked-after children, but they try, wherever possible, to place children with a foster family. Children in the care system often feel emotionally vulnerable and can have challenging behaviour. The NSPCC and the Who Cares? Trust provide advice and help for children in care to support them in achieving their full potential.

References

National Society for the Prevention of Cruelty to Children (NSPCC) http://www.nspcc.org.uk

The Who Cares? Trust http://www.thewhocarestrust.org.uk

Communication

Early years practitioners must be skilful communicators. They need to understand how children develop communication skills and the many diverse ways that children communicate at different stages of their development. Some children may be learning English as an additional language and some children may have additional language needs.

Developing children's communication

Learning language is a complex process, which is influenced by many factors. Early years practitioners need to understand this process to provide support for children's developing communication.

Babies learn language by observing, listening to and interacting with others. The term 'motherese' (also known as 'parentese' or 'baby talk') describes the way that most adults talk to young babies. It is characterised by a 'cooing' pattern of intonation and an emphasis on important words. Research has shown that 'motherese' helps babies to receive clear signals about how language works. Early years practitioners need to engage with babies in playful, conversational exchanges.

As children become more competent language users, practitioners can continue to provide support for children's developing communication by:

➤ providing a 'language-rich' environment with stimulating interactions, activities and experiences

➤ using positive body language

➤ listening actively and giving children time to respond

➤ modelling appropriate language and consistently being a good role model

➤ expanding on children's communication and adding new vocabulary.

Case in point

Aleena works in the toddler room at Little Angels Nursery and she is the key person for Jennifer, aged 20 months. A recent conversation between Jennifer (J) and Aleena (A) went like this:

J: "Car."

A: "Yes, it's a blue car." (nodding, with a big smile)

J: "Brm, brm."

A: "The car goes brm, brm." (moves the toy car on the mat)

J: "Dadda car."

A: "Your daddy has a blue car." (smiles and points at the toy car)

J: "Bu car."

A: "Yes, your daddy has a blue car. Clever girl, Jennifer!" (gives Jennifer a big smile and a hug)

In this conversation, Aleena is supporting Jennifer's communication by using positive body language and praise, modelling appropriate language and expanding on Jennifer's communication efforts by adding new vocabulary.

Supporting children with additional language needs

Some children may experience communication problems such as delayed language development or pronunciation difficulties. In most cases, these will be temporary, but a small number of children will have more severe or permanent difficulties, requiring specific support through speech and language therapy. Some children may need to use enhanced methods of communication such as Makaton, Picture Exchange Communication System (PECS) or other systems of sign language.

Supporting English language learners

There are many children in early years settings across the UK whose home language is not English. These children can present a number of communication challenges and early years practitioners must provide appropriate support. Bilingualism is an asset and research suggests that children need to develop and use their home language. The cognitive skills involved in using one language are transferable to learning new languages, giving children knowledge about how language works and supporting both their developing skills in English and their confidence.

Additional visual support is vital for children learning English and practitioners should use a variety of practical resources such as pictures, symbols and play activities to support children's communication. A bilingual support worker may work with children in the setting and this helps to develop a relationship with the child and their family.

Summary

Effective communication is an essential part of working with children. Early years practitioners need to provide a 'language-rich environment' with opportunities for children to develop their competence in communicating, speaking and listening. Practitioners should be familiar with the language(s) that children use at home and make positive links with the family.

Reference

I Can (the children's communication charity) http://www.ican.org.uk

Conception

New human life is created through the process of conception, in which a female ovum (egg) is fertilised by a male sperm. Both the male and female reproductive systems must be functioning effectively for conception to take place. Contraception describes methods that can be used to prevent conception taking place.

Genetics and conception

Genetics is the study of heredity and inherited characteristics. Children inherit genes from both parents and these determine characteristics such as hair colour and blood group. Genes are carried on chromosomes and every normal human cell has 23 pairs of chromosomes, except the sperm and ovum which have 23 individual chromosomes.

When sperm and egg cells form, the sex chromosomes (XX for females and XY for males) are separated. This means that all egg cells carry a single X chromosome and sperm cells carry either an X or a Y chromosome. The gender of a baby is therefore determined by what kind of sperm (X or Y) fertilises the egg.

Occasionally, genetic malformations occur, resulting in conditions such as Down's syndrome, when individuals have 47 chromosomes instead of 46 (see *Atypical development*). Some genes carry defects that may cause inherited disorders such as cystic fibrosis or haemophilia.

Infertility

There are many reasons why conception may not take place. It can result from problems with either the male or the female reproductive systems but can also occur for no obvious physical reason. Some reasons for infertility include:

➤ Hormone imbalance

➤ Blocked Fallopian tubes

➤ Low sperm count.

There are several kinds of infertility treatment, but one of the most commonly used is *in vitro* fertilisation (IVF). This is a complex medical procedure that involves removing ripened ova (eggs) from the female and fertilising them with male sperm in controlled laboratory conditions. The fertilised ova are then implanted into the female uterus and, if successful, at least one fertilised ovum will develop into an embryo. This procedure may result in the birth of twins or multiple babies.

Twins

Occasionally, conception may result in twins or multiple embryos developing.

Identical twins are conceived when the fertilised ovum splits into two and develops into two embryos. Identical twins are also called uniovular twins (from one ovum) and are always the same gender.

Non-identical twins are conceived when two ova are released at the same time and both become fertilised by different sperm. They develop into two embryos, also known as fraternal or binovular twins (from two ova), and can be either the same gender or different.

Methods of contraception

Planning whether to have a baby, or not, is an important decision and the use of contraception is part of this process. There are many different methods of contraception for both men and women, and some are more effective and reliable than others. Some of the more reliable methods include:

➤ Male condoms

➤ Contraceptive pills ('combined' pill or progesterone only)

➤ Male vasectomy or female sterilisation

➤ Abstention (not having sexual intercourse).

Barrier methods of contraception, like condoms, also provide some protection against sexually transmitted diseases, such as gonorrhoea or the human immuno-deficiency virus (HIV).

Other reliable methods of contraception include:

➤ Female condoms and diaphragm (cap)

➤ Contraceptive injections and implants

➤ Intrauterine devices (IUDs).

Summary

The process of conception is an important part of human development. It is at this early stage that the sex of the baby is determined and inherited characteristics are established. Conception can result in the development of twins. Sometimes infertility can lead to the inability to conceive. The wide range of contraceptive methods available enables couples to make rational decisions about when to have a baby.

Concepts

Concepts are the ideas that form the building blocks of children's knowledge. As children start to make connections between their experiences, they gradually learn to organise their thinking so that it makes sense, a process which involves understanding about concepts. The ability to understand concepts develops over time and gradually children begin to figure out how different concepts link together as they develop problem-solving skills.

Concepts and cognitive development

Children's understanding of different concepts progresses with each stage of their cognitive development. From about the age of nine months, babies begin to understand that objects still exist even though they cannot see them (this is known as the concept of object permanence); for example, babies enjoy the game of 'peep-o', knowing that the person will disappear and reappear. Young children begin to understand simple, concrete concepts such as colour, size and shape when they recognise the difference between 'red' and 'blue', 'big' and 'small', 'round' and 'square'. Older children understand more complex abstract concepts such as time, mass and volume.

Abstract concepts

Abstract concepts, such as happiness, sadness, anger or death, are more difficult for children to understand because they do not have a physical reference and are not concrete or tangible. Many mathematical concepts are abstract and teachers need to use concrete representations to help children understand, for example by cutting up an apple to explain the mathematical concept of fractions. With reference to Piaget's stages of cognitive development, children struggle to fully understand many abstract concepts until the formal operational stage, around the age of 10 years (see *Theories*).

Case in point

Maggie is five years old and her mother recently died from cancer. She tells her teacher at school: "My mummy got sick and she died, but I hope she will be back before my birthday."

This highlights Maggie's limited understanding of the abstract concept of death. Although she can confidently talk about her mother being sick and subsequently dying, she does not yet understand that death is permanent.

Mia is three years old and is very excited about her birthday in five days' time. Her mother knows that Mia does not understand the concept of time and so she tells Mia that her birthday will be here after five 'big sleeps'. She helps Mia to cross the dates off a chart each day. This gives Mia something concrete to support her in understanding the concept of time.

Summary

Understanding concepts is an important part of children's cognitive development. This starts at an early age as children learn through their play and gradually build on their experiences to extend their ideas and thinking skills.

Confidentiality

The term 'confidentiality' relates to the duty of practitioners to handle personal information in ways that are appropriate, safe and meet legal requirements. 'Confidential' means 'private'. Early years practitioners who work with children and families are frequently in possession of information that is sensitive and private, for example from face-to-face conversations, telephone messages, written reports or electronic information.

The importance of confidentiality

Building relationships with children and their families is essential to developing trust. If practitioners share personal and private information about families with others who have no need or right to know, they risk breaking that trust.

Some information must be kept confidential (private) to protect children's safety. For example, a child's welfare might be put at risk if an abusive parent is made aware of the child's address through a breach in confidentiality. Early years settings have a legal requirement to manage and safeguard personal information correctly and should have a confidentiality policy (see *Policies and procedures*).

Protecting confidential information

Personal records, including notes, reports and letters concerning individual children and their families, should always be kept in a lockable filing cabinet. Paper documents, diaries and telephone messages should never be left lying around if they contain confidential information. Computers should be protected using authorised passwords and care should be taken when transferring information using portable memory devices.

In early years settings, practitioners should discuss sensitive or personal information in a private place. Confidential information should never be discussed over the telephone and confidential messages should never be left on an answering machine. Early years practitioners should always act in a professional manner and never gossip about children and their families, including on social media sites.

Legal requirements

There is no specific privacy law in the UK, but issues relating to privacy and confidentiality are incorporated into some legislation, for example the Data Protection Act 1998 and the Freedom of Information Act 2005. Some of these legal requirements include:

➤ Only obtaining information that is relevant to your requirements

➤ Not disclosing information to others unless there is a legitimate reason

➤ Keeping personal information up to date and not keeping records longer than necessary

➤ Keeping information in a safe place.

Sharing information

Information sharing amongst professionals who work with children and their families is essential. It enables everyone to work in the best interests of the child, particularly in potentially abusive situations. However, it is important that information is shared on a 'need to know' basis and that the purpose of sharing the information is clearly defined. Parental consent should always be obtained before sharing any information with other professionals (see *Parents as partners*).

Confidential information should only be disclosed when the safety or wellbeing of a child is threatened (see *Multi-agency working*).

Case in point

Julie works at Bright Stars Nursery. As the children are leaving at the end of the day, one of the parents, Mrs Smith, asks Julie for the telephone number of another parent so that she can invite her child to a birthday party. Julie informs Mrs Smith that she cannot disclose that information as it would breach the setting's confidentiality policy.

The next morning Julie answers the telephone in the setting and the caller states that he is a speech and language therapist. He asks for the personal details of one of the children in the setting. Julie asks the caller for his contact details and says that she will call back. She then checks with her manager before taking any further action.

Summary

There is a legal requirement to protect the privacy of children and their families, and practitioners have a responsibility to work within these guidelines. Early years settings should have a confidentiality policy that includes procedures about the recording, storage and sharing of personal information.

Reference

Data Protection Act 1998 (c. 29). London: The Stationery Office.
http://www.legislation.gov.uk

Cot death

Cot death (Sudden Infant Death Syndrome) is a term commonly used to describe a sudden and unexpected infant death that is initially unexplained (Lullaby Trust). In the majority of cases, there is no identifiable cause of death, but it is likely that a combination of factors affect babies at a vulnerable stage of their development.

The incidence of cot death

In the UK, over 300 babies die every year as a result of Sudden Infant Death Syndrome and 72 per cent of all unexplained deaths occur in babies aged less than four months (Lullaby Trust, 2012). More babies die as a result of cot death each year than from road traffic accidents, leukaemia and meningitis combined. Cot deaths usually occur when a baby is sleeping during the night, but can occur anywhere at any time. Research has shown that babies born with a low birth weight are four times more likely to die as a result of cot death than babies born with a normal birth weight (see *Prematurity*).

Reducing the risk of cot death

The Lullaby Trust has outlined a number of measures which can be taken to reduce the risk of cot death, including:

➤ Do not smoke during pregnancy.

➤ Do not let anyone smoke in the same room as the baby.

➤ Always place babies on their back to sleep, with their feet at the foot of the cot to prevent them wriggling under the covers.

➤ Never use a pillow or duvet in the baby's cot.

➤ Have the baby's cot in the parents' room for the first six months of life.

➤ Do not let babies get too hot and keep their head uncovered when sleeping.

➤ Never sleep with a baby on a sofa or in the same bed, to reduce the risk of suffocation.

➤ Breast-feed the baby.

➤ Use a dummy to settle the baby to sleep.

Summary

The sudden and unexpected death of a baby is one of the most distressing events that can ever happen. Research has shown that a number of factors can contribute towards the risk of cot death. However, evidence from the Lullaby Trust has shown that by changing patterns of infant care, the risk of cot death can be considerably reduced.

Reference

The Lullaby Trust (2012) *Evidence Base*. http://www.lullabytrust.org.uk

Creative, critical thinking

Creative, critical thinking is when children explore their ideas and make connections. Babies and young children explore and investigate through their play and become absorbed by what they can do with different objects and materials, as long as these are suitable for their stage of development. These investigations help children to develop an understanding of different situations and make sense of their environment.

The development of creative, critical thinking

Children will investigate and explore with intense concentration, making connections and developing their own ideas. For example, babies will investigate items in a treasure basket using their senses and will find out how objects feel or sound and what they can do with them (see *Play resources*). As children develop and become more mobile, they extend their creative, critical thinking through:

➤ exploring and using information, for example in heuristic play (see *Play resources*)

➤ planning, predicting and thinking ahead

➤ solving problems, working things out and finding solutions (see *Active learning*)

➤ using logic, explaining and noticing cause and effect

➤ imagining new situations, fantasising and creating.

Supporting creative, critical thinking

Practitioners can help children to make connections in their play and learning, for example by encouraging them to express their ideas through music, dance, painting, puppets and role-play. They can also provide opportunities for children to capture and represent their ideas using digital media or storytelling, and by providing imaginative resources both inside the setting and outdoors.

Children need time to process information and practitioners should use open-ended questioning to engage children in sustained, shared thinking (see *Learning through play*). Setting problems for children to solve will develop their creativity and critical thinking. Communicating with parents will help practitioners to find out about children's interests at home and build on these ideas to stimulate creativity and curiosity.

Case in point

Jessica, aged four years, is fascinated when she finds a fly caught in a spider's web in the nursery garden. She calls the practitioner over to look.

Jessica: "Look!"

Practitioner: "Ooh, the spider has caught a fly in its web."

Jessica: "It's trapped."

Practitioner: "Yes, it's like a net, for the spider to catch its food."

Jessica: "It doesn't fall off."

Practitioner: "I wonder why?"

Jessica: "It's all tied up, it can't escape."

Practitioner: "Yes, it's stuck in the web. What might happen now?"

Jessica: "Where's the spider?"

Practitioner: "Let's have a look, shall we?" (takes out a magnifying glass and together they examine the web)

Jessica: "There's the spider, on the edge."

Practitioner: "Yes, it's waiting to pounce!"

Jessica: "And eat the fly!"

The practitioner is supporting Jessica's creative, critical thinking by helping her to express her ideas and make connections. She asks open-ended questions and engages Jessica in sustained, shared thinking. The practitioner may develop this with Jessica by encouraging her to take photographs or draw pictures and create a story about the spider in the web.

Summary

Creativity develops when children are given the opportunity to become absorbed in exploring the world around them (DfE, 2012). Creativity fosters critical thinking by allowing children to make connections, review their ideas and adapt their knowledge and understanding. Early years practitioners can support creative, critical thinking by encouraging children to explore their environment, investigate new situations and process information. This enables children to explore possibilities, develop their ideas and discover new meanings.

References

Department for Education (2012) *Statutory Framework for the Early Years Foundation Stage*. http://www.education.gov.uk

Foundation Years http://www.foundationyears.org.uk

Cross-infection

Cross-infection is the transfer and spread of harmful organisms, such as bacteria and viruses, from one person to another. Young children are vulnerable to infection as their immune systems are still developing. Early years practitioners need to understand how infection spreads and should take precautions to protect children's health.

The spread of infection

In early years settings, infection can spread in a variety of ways, including:

➤ Airborne (or droplet): infection spreads through the air by coughing or sneezing.

➤ Direct contact (skin to skin): infection spreads through touching.

➤ Ingestion (swallowing): infection can be spread by eating contaminated food or touching food with dirty hands.

➤ Body fluids: some infections, such as HIV, can spread from one person to another by direct exchange of body fluids (e.g. blood).

➤ Vectors: some infections can be spread by animals and insects (e.g. flies).

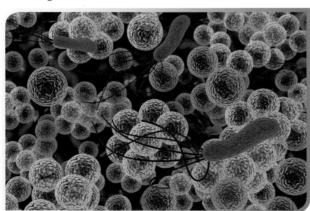

Preventing the spread of infection

Early years practitioners have a responsibility to minimise the spread of infection by setting a good example with young children and following strict procedures (see *Policies and procedures*).

The statutory safeguarding and welfare requirements of the Early Years Foundation Stage clearly state: *'Providers must keep premises and equipment clean, and be aware of, and comply with, requirements of health and safety legislation (including hygiene requirements)'* (DfE, 2012).

Some of the ways to prevent the spread of infection include:

➤ Having good ventilation in the setting

➤ Covering the mouth when coughing or sneezing

➤ Using tissues and disposing of them appropriately

➤ Encouraging thorough hand-washing procedures (particularly after using the toilet, before handling food and after touching animals or playing outside)

➤ Having strict food hygiene procedures

➤ Covering any cuts with waterproof, adhesive dressings

➤ Cleaning and disinfecting equipment, toys and play materials regularly

➤ Wearing disposable aprons and gloves when dealing with blood and other body fluids (including changing nappies)

➤ Disposing of nappies and other waste materials appropriately.

Notifying relevant authorities

Cases of some infectious diseases in early years settings must be reported to Ofsted (or the equivalent regulatory organisation). The outbreak of some infectious diseases (such as meningitis) must be reported to the Health Protection Agency (HPA). Early years practitioners must report and record all information accurately and provide clear information and reassurance for parents (see *Recording and reporting*).

Summary

Preventing the spread of infection is extremely important for protecting children from illness and promoting good health. In early years settings where there are groups of children together, infection can easily spread from one child to another. This can be minimised if early years practitioners follow guidelines, use equipment correctly and encourage children to do the same.

Reference

Department for Education (2012) *Statutory Framework for the Early Years Foundation Stage*. http://www.education.gov.uk

Curriculum frameworks

The statutory requirements for early education in the UK are outlined through specific curriculum frameworks. These provide a structure for children's learning and development in the early years and help practitioners to plan meaningful experiences and activities.

Regional variations

England, Scotland, Wales and Northern Ireland all have their own curriculum frameworks. For example, in England, the Statutory Framework for the Early Years Foundation Stage (EYFS) (see *EYFS*) outlines the learning and development requirements for children from birth to five years old. In Wales, the Foundation Phase for Children's Learning outlines the requirements for children aged three to seven years old. All schools and Ofsted-registered early years providers must follow the EYFS, including childminders, pre-schools, nurseries and school reception classes. Once children reach compulsory school age, all four countries of the UK follow a National Curriculum, for example the Curriculum for Excellence in Scotland and the Northern Ireland Primary Curriculum.

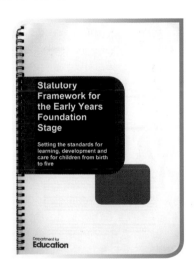

Statutory Framework for the Early Years Foundation Stage

Setting the standards for learning, development and care for children from birth to five

Department for Education

Alternative curriculum frameworks

Some early years settings follow specific curriculum frameworks, which have been influenced by famous educational pioneers. These alternative curriculum approaches include the following:

➤ Maria Montessori (1870–1952) was born in Italy and developed the Montessori method of educating children. She believed that each child is born with a unique potential to be revealed. Part of the Montessori method emphasises the importance of 'practical life' activities, which support children in working independently to develop concentration and self-discipline. The practitioner facilitates children's learning and 'follows the child'.

➤ Rudolf Steiner (1861–1925) was born in Austria and developed Steiner Waldorf Education. This grew out of his spiritual research ('anthroposophy') and is based on a deep understanding of human development that respects a secure and unhurried childhood. Steiner Waldorf Education addresses the needs of the whole child and emphasises self-motivated enquiry. The practitioner is a model rather than an instructor and promotes creative, sensory experiences within a secure daily routine.

Influences on curriculum frameworks

The following influences have shaped the provision of early education in settings across the UK:

➤ Reggio Emilia pre-schools are named after their place of origin in northern Italy. The Reggio Emilia philosophy emphasises the interdependence of social and individual learning and this has influenced the planning and provision of activities and experiences within the EYFS. The environment is seen as 'the third teacher' and real life experiences provide the context for children to investigate their ideas and be active in their own learning. Children are encouraged to express their creativity in a variety of different ways.

➤ Te Whariki is the curriculum framework in New Zealand for children from birth to six years. The philosophy of this approach has influenced the EYFS framework and the focus on children's individual needs and enthusiasms. The curriculum is based on the four principles of empowerment, holistic development, family and community, and relationships.

➤ The High Scope approach uses the process of 'active participatory learning' and promotes independence, curiosity, decision-making and problem-solving. A key component of this approach is the 'Plan-Do-Review' routine, in which children construct their own learning through expressing an intention, generating a learning experience and reflecting on the outcomes. This has influenced the importance of children's active learning in early years curriculum frameworks.

➤ The Forest School movement is an outdoor approach to play and education, supporting children's learning about the natural environment, risk management, problem-solving and cooperation. This has influenced the approach to outdoor learning, particularly within the EYFS.

Summary

Curriculum frameworks provide guidance and support for early years practitioners. There are many different approaches across the UK and a variety of influences have helped to shape the provision in early years settings.

References

Community Playthings http://www.communityplaythings.co.uk/learning-library/articles/reggio-emilia

Department for Education http://www.education.gov.uk

Education Scotland http://www.educationscotland.gov.uk

Forest Schools http://www.forestschools.com

High Scope http://www.highscope.org

Montessori Education (UK) http://www.montessorieducationuk.org

Northern Ireland Curriculum http://www.nicurriculum.org.uk

Steiner Waldorf Schools Fellowship http://www.steinerwaldorf.org

Welsh Government http://www.wales.gov.uk

Development in-utero

Development in-utero refers to the development of the foetus during pregnancy when it is in the uterus (womb). This is one of the most rapid periods in child development. It begins with conception and continues for the duration of full-term pregnancy (usually 37 to 42 weeks). Pregnancy is divided into three different periods (trimesters), and specific milestones in the baby's development mark each stage.

The first trimester

The first trimester (the first 12 weeks of pregnancy) is one of the most critical times in the pregnancy. The fertilised ovum embeds into the lining of the uterus (the process of implantation), where the embryo begins to grow and develop. During this period, the developing embryo is most vulnerable to influences from harmful substances, such as drugs or infections (see *Antenatal provision*).

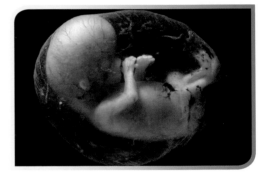

By the sixth week, the embryo has a beating heart and limb buds show where the arms and legs are developing. From the eighth week, the embryo is referred to as a foetus and by 12 weeks, an average foetus measures 6 cm (2.5 in) and weighs 9–14 g (0.5 oz).

Most of the major body organs are formed during the first trimester, although they will need more time to reach full maturity.

The second trimester

The second trimester (weeks 12 to 25) of the pregnancy is a period of rapid growth. The foetus is now moving about vigorously and from about week 20 the pregnant woman can usually feel the foetus kicking. The skin of the foetus is covered in a white greasy substance (vernix) and fine hair (lanugo). This provides protection for the baby's skin as it floats in the amniotic fluid. By 24 weeks, the foetus is considered to be viable, that is able to survive on its own outside of the uterus. Most babies born before this time cannot live because their lungs and other vital organs are not sufficiently developed. At 25 weeks, an average foetus measures 21 cm (8 in) and weighs around 700 g (1.5 lb).

The third trimester

During the third trimester (from week 25 to full term) of the pregnancy, the foetus grows very rapidly in preparation for birth and life outside of the uterus. Towards the end of this trimester, the baby will settle low in the uterus with the head facing downwards (engaged). Occasionally, the baby will settle with its bottom, legs or feet facing downwards (breech position), but in most cases it will turn around before the birth. At full term, an average baby measures 50 cm (20 in) and weighs 3.5 kg (7 lb 7 oz).

Summary

Each new human life develops from a single cell, which multiplies and grows into body systems and organs. Pregnancy progresses through three trimesters and the baby grows and develops at a very rapid rate. Most of the baby's major body organs are formed during the first trimester and they continue to grow and mature during the second and third trimesters in preparation for birth. Development in-utero is one of the most important stages of child development.

Diversity

Diversity refers to the differences between people. Early years practitioners work with people from a wide range of social, cultural and ethnic backgrounds, including people of different genders, people with disabilities or people who have different cultural traditions. They have a responsibility to embrace and value diversity in order to meet the individual needs of children and their families. Discrimination is the unequal treatment of a person or group based on prejudice.

Embracing diversity

All children are unique individuals. In early years settings, practitioners must ensure that each child is valued and respected equally by actively celebrating differences, embracing diversity and exploring the rich culture we live in (see *Inclusive practice*). They might include specific activities to promote a positive attitude towards diversity, for example by:

➤ providing dolls from different ethnicities and musical instruments from different countries and traditions

➤ displaying positive images that embrace diversity, including children with disabilities and both boys and girls from different countries

➤ sharing stories that explore and celebrate differences between people

➤ celebrating special days connected with a range of faiths, including traditional food and customs

➤ providing dressing-up clothes representing different ethnic or religious cultures, such as a sari, hijab or yarmulke

➤ learning Makaton or other sign language with all the children in the setting

➤ adapting the physical environment of the setting so that children of all abilities or disabilities can access the facilities easily

➤ showing equal respect for all children, parents and families who visit the setting.

Discrimination and prejudice

Diversity is not welcomed or celebrated by everyone and this can result in discrimination (the unequal treatment of a person or group). This may happen because of a child's skin colour, physical characteristics, disability, social background, religion, culture or way of life.

Prejudice is often the cause of unfair discrimination. A prejudice is an opinion or attitude of dislike towards another individual or group of people and is often based on inaccurate information. Prejudice is often expressed through taunting behaviour such as derogatory name-calling or drawing attention to physical differences such as skin colour or facial features. Prejudicial behaviour and discrimination can lead to negative stereotypes and unfair treatment. Early years practitioners must avoid prejudice by being knowledgeable  about different cultures, acknowledging diversity and discouraging stereotyping (making assumptions about an individual because of their background or needs).

Challenging discrimination

Discrimination can be very damaging to children and their families. Early years practitioners should actively challenge any incidence of discriminatory practice that they witness, including:

➤ Intervening when children, families or other staff use discriminatory language or behaviour and being clear that it is not acceptable

➤ Providing accurate information to enable individuals to use appropriate language and behaviour

➤ Providing support for children who have been subjected to discrimination.

Early years practitioners have to work within a framework of legislation, policies and procedures that are designed to promote equality and prevent discrimination (see *Policies and procedures*). The Childcare Act 2006 and the Equality Act 2010 actively promote anti-discriminatory practice, protecting individual rights and banning unfair treatment.

Summary

Acknowledging diversity, confronting prejudice and challenging all forms of discrimination are important aspects of professional practice in early years settings. Equality for all children and families requires a commitment to anti-discriminatory practice and an awareness of situations that may lead to a lack of fairness. Early years practitioners have a responsibility to meet the needs of all children and families through inclusive practice and the provision of equal opportunities.

Reference

Equality Act 2010 (c. 15). London: The Stationery Office. http://www.legislation.gov.uk

Early intervention

'Early intervention' is the term used to describe the process of identifying potential problems in children's development as early as possible. The purpose of intervening (becoming involved) early is to prevent problems developing or to reduce the severity of problems that have started to emerge. It might include referral or signposting to other services and can occur at any point in a child's life.

Reasons for early intervention

There are many reasons why children may be involved in the early intervention process and be referred for specialist assessment, treatment or care, including:

➤ atypical development, particularly developmental delay (see *Atypical development*)

➤ health problems

➤ communication difficulties

➤ social, emotional or behavioural difficulties

➤ learning difficulties or special educational needs (see *SEN*)

➤ concerns about children's safety or welfare (see *Safeguarding*).

Children may be referred to more than one specialist for assessment or services. For example, a child with Autistic Spectrum Disorder (ASD) might be referred to a speech and language therapist, an educational psychologist and a behavioural support specialist.

If potential problems are identified at an early stage, then action can be taken to prevent more serious difficulties occurring. The Common Assessment Framework (CAF) helps practitioners to make a holistic assessment of children's needs and identify what support is needed (see *Multi-agency working*).

The referral process

A referral is a recommendation for an individual to receive specialist care or services. In the early years sector, this usually involves a professional making a request for a child to be assessed or to receive more expert care. For example, a health visitor may have concerns about a child's speech following a routine developmental assessment. The health visitor would then discuss this with the parents and make a referral to the speech and language therapist. This information needs to be shared in order to provide the best support for the child and their family (see *Multi-agency working*).

Case in point

Mrs Jones is concerned about the developmental progress of her son, Ralph, who is 15 months old. He can sit up without support and crawl around, but he has made no attempt to pull himself up or try to walk. Ralph communicates by babbling and does not use any recognisable words.

The health visitor at the local Children's Centre carries out some developmental checks on Ralph and discusses Mrs Jones's concerns. She decides to refer Ralph to the specialist child development unit at the children's hospital for a full physical examination and assessment by a paediatrician. He will also have a hearing test at the audiology clinic and a speech and language assessment by the speech and language therapist.

All the professionals involved will share the results of their investigations with each other and with Mrs Jones. As a result of this referral, a plan will be developed to provide specialist services to support Ralph and his family.

This early intervention could minimise further developmental problems for Ralph and prevent more serious speech and language difficulties, which could affect his future development and learning.

Summary

The early intervention process enables professionals to identify children's specific needs, highlight areas of difficulty and initiate any specialist treatment or care that may be required. Research has shown that intervening early can make a significant difference in reducing the incidence of more serious problems and improving outcomes for children and their families.

Reference

STEARNS, J., SCHMIEDER, C. & MILLAR, E. (2011) Level 3 Diploma for the Children and Young People's Workforce: Early Learning and Childcare. London: HarperCollins Publishers.

Early years sector

The early years sector is a term used to describe the early years providers and the professional workforce in early years. This includes the providers of full-day and sessional childcare, children's centres and out-of-school care in addition to childminders and primary schools. The early years sector is supported by Skills for Care and Development (SfC&D), which is the sector skills council for people working in early years.

The early years workforce

The professional workforce in the early years sector consists of people working in early years and children's services. Practitioners work in a wide variety of employment roles, for example as nursery practitioners, teaching assistants, childminders and supporting children with special educational needs.

The SfC&D recognises that the quality of staff and their qualification levels are strongly associated with good quality provision. This is currently being addressed through the Nutbrown review (see *Career development*).

Early years providers

The early years sector has undergone a considerable transformation in the past decade, both in terms of the range of providers who offer childcare services, and also in the number of places available. Providers within the early years sector are generally grouped as follows:

➤ Full-day childcare (e.g. a day nursery)

➤ Sessional childcare (e.g. a pre-school or playgroup)

➤ After-school and holiday care (out-of-school care)

➤ Children's centres

➤ Childminders

➤ Primary schools with reception/nursery classes

➤ Nursery schools.

Types of provision

Provision for children and families within the early years sector includes statutory as well as private and voluntary services.

Statutory services have to be provided by law through government organisations such as local authorities. In the early years sector these services are usually referred to as 'maintained provision', for example primary schools.

Private and voluntary services are independent of the government and are provided by a range of private organisations, volunteers and self-employed practitioners:

➤ Private sector services include day nurseries and independent schools. Registered childminders are the largest group of self-employed practitioners.

➤ The voluntary early years sector consists of large national organisations, such as the NSPCC, in addition to small voluntary groups who provide playgroups and other support groups for children and families.

Integrated children's services

Part of the statutory provision in the early years sector combines health, social care and early years provision to create an integrated service for children and families. Children's centres provide the focus for many integrated services, bringing together childcare, early education, health and family support services and helping to improve the health, welfare and long-term outcomes for children and their families.

Summary

The early years sector is made up of a very diverse workforce. Professionals provide care and early education in children's centres, schools, nurseries or in a home-based environment. Early years and children's services are provided in statutory, private and voluntary settings, and integrated services combine health, social care and early years provision within the early years sector.

References

Department for Education http://www.education.gov.uk

Skills for Care and Development http://www.skillsforcareanddevelopment. org.uk

Egocentric

The term 'egocentric' refers to children's inability to see a situation from another person's point of view. Up to a certain age, young children are completely focused on their own needs and do not understand that other people have needs that are different from their own. This affects children's thinking and behaviour, and makes it very difficult for young children to understand the feelings of others.

Piaget's experiments

Jean Piaget was very interested in children's thinking processes (see *Theories*). According to Piaget, the egocentric child assumes that other people see, hear and feel exactly the same as the child does. He wanted to find out at what age children's egocentric thinking disappeared.

Piaget demonstrated this using a three-dimensional model of three mountains, with different objects on each peak. He placed a doll at various points around the model and gave the child several pictures showing different views of the mountains. Piaget then asked the child to choose which picture showed what the doll could see (the doll's view).

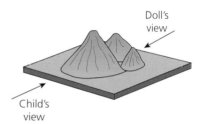

Doll's view

Child's view

Piaget discovered that children up to the age of seven years (in the pre-operational stage) would choose the picture showing what they could see (not what the doll could see). Children over the age of seven years (in the concrete operational stage) would choose the correct picture. Piaget concluded from his experiment that by the age of seven years, children's thinking is no longer egocentric because they can see more than their own point of view.

One of the key strengths of Piaget's work is that it helps to explain children's development of logical thought. However, one of the main criticisms is that his theories focus on age trends in cognitive development, with very little emphasis on the process of learning, or on how children move from one stage to the next.

Piaget's theories have also since been criticised for being based on too small a sample of children and situations. It is now believed that, in general, children are able to see from others' points of view earlier than Piaget thought.

Relevance to early years practice

Early years practitioners need to fully understand young children's egocentric thinking and behaviour. When children are totally focused on their own needs, they have little regard for the needs of others around them. Egocentrism affects children's ability to play cooperatively, share their toys and understand different situations and viewpoints. This is a normal stage in children's development and practitioners need to appreciate this in order to have realistic expectations of young children.

Case in point

1. Gemma is four years old and her mother has tragically been killed in a car accident. When Gemma's family gathers to tell her what has happened, her response is to say, "Well, who is going to take me to ballet now?"

Gemma is demonstrating egocentrism, because her primary concern is for her own needs and she has a very limited understanding of the concept of death.

2. Robbie is three years old and his mother has just had a new baby girl, so she has less free time to spend with Robbie. Robbie responds to this by demanding his mother's attention, screaming and jumping on the furniture. He is sometimes aggressive with the new baby and makes her cry.

Robbie is demonstrating egocentrism, because he is totally focused on his own needs and cannot understand that the new baby has needs, which are different from his own (see *Regression*).

Summary

Although Piaget's experiments have been criticised, it is important to recognise the significance of these studies in the overall understanding of children's egocentric thinking. Early years practitioners need to be aware of this stage in children's development in order to fully understand children's thinking and behaviour.

EYFS

The Statutory Framework for the Early Years Foundation Stage (EYFS) was introduced in England in September 2008 and revised in 2012. It sets out the standards that all early years providers must legally meet to ensure that children learn and develop well and are kept healthy and safe (DfE, 2012). It consists of both the statutory safeguarding and welfare requirements, and the learning and development recommendations.

Main principles

The EYFS specifies requirements for safeguarding and promoting children's welfare, from birth to five years of age, and recommendations for children's learning and development. The overarching principles of the EYFS are:

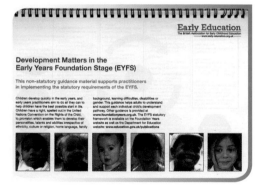

➤ Every child is unique, capable and constantly learning.

➤ Children learn to be strong and independent through positive relationships.

➤ Children learn and develop well in enabling environments where there is a strong partnership between practitioners and parents.

➤ Children develop and learn in different ways and at different rates.

The learning and development recommendations

The EYFS learning and development recommendations consist of seven key areas of learning and development: three prime areas and four specific areas.

The three prime areas are:

➤ **Personal, social and emotional development:** enabling children to develop a positive sense of themselves, form positive relationships and learn how to manage their feelings and behaviour

➤ **Communication and language:** enabling children to develop their skills in speaking, listening and expressing themselves

➤ **Physical development:** enabling children to develop their coordination and understand the importance of physical activity and healthy eating.

The four specific areas are:

➤ **Literacy:** enabling children to link sounds and letters and begin to read and write

➤ **Mathematics:** enabling children to develop skills in counting, using numbers, and understanding shape, space and measure

➤ **Understanding the world:** enabling children to make sense of their physical world, explore their community and find out about people, places, technology and the environment

➤ **Expressive arts and design:** enabling children to explore and play with a wide range of media and share their ideas and feelings through art, music, dance and role-play.

Monitoring children's progress

Observation is the primary tool for noting children's progress in the EYFS. Regular, ongoing observation enables practitioners to check children's progress towards the early learning goals. These goals outline the milestones in learning and development that most children should be expected to achieve by the end of the foundation stage (usually at the end of Year R in schools, at the age of five years).

Progress of children in the EYFS is measured by the two-year-old progress check and through the Early Years Foundation Stage Profile (EYFSP). Practitioners must review the progress of children between the ages of two and three years, and provide a short written summary for their parents. The EYFSP must be completed for every child at the end of the foundation stage. This Profile provides parents and teachers with a well-rounded picture of a child's abilities and their readiness for starting school (see *Recording and reporting*).

The safeguarding and welfare requirements

The safeguarding and welfare requirements identify the steps that early years providers must take to keep children safe and promote their welfare. These requirements include guidance on:

➤ **Child protection:** including safeguarding policies and procedures to keep children safe from harm (see *Safeguarding*)

➤ **Suitable people:** to ensure that people looking after children are fit for the requirements of their roles

➤ **Children's health:** including responding to children who are ill, taking necessary steps to prevent the spread of infection and the provision of first aid treatment

➤ **Food and drink:** including the provision of healthy, nutritious meals, snacks and drinks and the management of children's special dietary requirements (see *Healthy eating*)

➤ **Safety and suitability of premises, environment and equipment:** to ensure children's safety and security, including health and hygiene, emergency procedures and risk assessment (see *Risk assessment*)

➤ **Information and records:** to maintain records and share information with parents, carers and other professionals working with the child (see *Recording and reporting*).

Case in point

The practitioners at Oaklands Nursery encourage children's learning and development across all seven areas of learning within the EYFS. They use circle time every day to encourage children to communicate with each other and express their feelings. They help children to make choices at snack time and encourage good manners and social interaction. The practitioners encourage children's physical skills with activities such as parachute games or action rhymes. Mathematics is supported through activities such as matching, sorting, making patterns, weighing, measuring and counting, and the children are encouraged to use mathematical language such as 'bigger than'. The children can extend their understanding of the world through experiencing nature outdoors or engaging with digital technology. Practitioners provide opportunities for children to dance, sing, make music and engage in different art projects. Literacy is encouraged through sharing books, stories, songs and rhymes and through activities to encourage mark-making with different tools.

Summary

The EYFS framework provides a set of common principles and commitments to deliver quality early education to all children from birth to five years old. It offers guidance for practitioners, quality and consistency for early years settings and a secure foundation for children through playing, exploring and active learning.

Reference

Department for Education (2012) *Statutory Framework for the Early Years Foundation Stage*. http://www.education.gov.uk

Family structures

A family is traditionally understood to be a group of people who live together or who are related. The family structure usually consists of one or more parents and at least one child. Family structures in the UK have become much more diverse as a result of social change, attitudes towards sexuality and an expanding multicultural population.

Types of family structure

Early years practitioners need to be aware of, and understand, the family structure of each child they are working with. There are many different types of family structure, including:

➤ Nuclear families, which consist of two heterosexual parents and their dependent children living together in the same household

➤ Extended families, which are nuclear families made larger by the presence of grandparents or other relatives living in the same household or neighbourhood

➤ One-parent families, which consist of a single parent (often the mother) and at least one dependent child

➤ Blended families (also known as reconstituted or step-families), which are families that have been re-formed, often as a result of divorce, and in many cases both parents bring children from previous relationships

➤ Same-sex families, which consist of same-sex partners (male or female) living with dependent children who may be their own offspring, adopted or fostered

➤ Adoptive families, which have at least one child who has been legally adopted by the parents. Adoption involves a legal process, which gives the adoptive parents full legal rights and responsibilities for the child

➤ Foster families, which are created when the parents of an existing family take on temporary fostering responsibility for a child who is unable to live in their own family. Foster parents have no legal rights over the child (see *Children in care*).

Case in point

One-parent family
Genine is a single mother with three children – two boys, aged seven and three years, and a girl, aged five years. She is divorced from the children's father, but he sees them on a regular basis.

Extended family
Jan and Olga are new immigrants to the UK from Poland. They have a five-month-old baby girl and an 18-month-old boy, and are currently living with Olga's elderly parents and Jan's uncle.

Blended family
Pam is 35 years old and divorced three years ago. Her new husband, Mike, has two sons from his previous marriage, who live with their mother in a neighbouring town. Pam has three children from her previous marriage, who all live with her and Mike.

Summary

Family structures have changed over time and families have become more diverse. However, regardless of the different ways in which it can be structured or organised, the family is still seen as the basic building block of society, and early years practitioners need to be aware of and be careful not to judge or discriminate against the many different variations in family structure.

Food hygiene

The concept of food hygiene describes the need to maintain high standards of cleanliness and correct storage of food. Safe food preparation is essential for children's health and wellbeing. Young children are vulnerable to infection and early years practitioners have a responsibility to maintain strict hygiene procedures when preparing food. In early years settings, all staff involved in preparing and handling food must receive training in food hygiene.

The importance of personal hygiene

Strict personal hygiene practice is very important when preparing food for children. This helps to minimise the spread of infection (see *Cross-infection*) and sets a good example to the children in the setting. Early years practitioners should always:

➤ wash their hands before touching food, after using the toilet and after handling anything dirty

➤ wear an apron and keep long hair tied back when preparing food for children

➤ cover any cuts with waterproof plasters

➤ avoid coughing or sneezing over food.

Children should be encouraged to develop good personal hygiene habits from an early age. Early years practitioners should support children with routines for hand washing before meals or snacks, after using the toilet and following any messy or outdoor play.

Food preparation and storage

The Food Standards Agency (FSA) operates in all four countries of the UK and outlines the regulations about food hygiene, including safe preparation and storage.

If strict hygiene regulations are not followed, food can become infected with harmful bacteria. This can result in food poisoning and other dangerous illnesses. Early years practitioners need to follow procedures for the preparation and storage of food in order to protect children's health, including:

➤ Always keep food covered.

➤ Keep the fridge at a temperature between 0 and 5°C.

➤ Clean and disinfect all food preparation surfaces regularly and always use clean utensils.

➤ Use separate utensils and chopping boards for raw meat and cooked foods.

➤ Wash fruit and vegetables before using them for snacks or meals.

➤ Always cook food thoroughly and avoid reheating food.

Strict hygiene procedures should always be followed when preparing food for babies (see *Infant feeding*). Infants have very little resistance to infection and are vulnerable to conditions such as gastroenteritis, which can be life-threatening. All the equipment for bottle feeds needs to be thoroughly sterilised and practitioners should:

➤ store bottle feeds in the fridge (but never for longer than 24 hours)

➤ never reheat any milk that is left in the bottle after a feed (it should always be thrown away)

➤ never use a microwave to warm bottle feeds.

Summary

The section on food hygiene in the Statutory Framework for the Early Years Foundation Stage requires that 'those responsible for preparing and handling food are competent to do so' (DfE, 2012). Everyone involved in preparing food for young children needs to understand the importance of food safety and hygiene and be aware of the procedures to protect children's health.

References

Department for Education (2012) *Statutory Framework for the Early Years Foundation Stage*. http://www.education.gov.uk

Food Standards Agency http://www.food.gov.uk

Healthy eating

Healthy eating refers to the need for children to eat a balanced diet to maintain their growth and development. Research has shown that healthy eating habits develop from a very young age and that unhealthy diets in childhood can lead to long-term health problems in later life. It is therefore very important to encourage children to develop sensible eating patterns right from the start.

A balanced diet

Children need to eat a variety of foods from the four main groups:

➤ Fruit and vegetables

➤ Bread, rice, potatoes, pasta and other starchy foods

➤ Meat, fish, eggs, beans and other non-dairy sources of protein

➤ Milk and dairy products.

They must also drink water.

All these foods contain nutrients that are essential for good health, for example protein, carbohydrate and vitamins. A healthy diet contains a balance of these nutrients, which all perform a different function in the body, for example protein for growth, carbohydrate for energy and vitamin C for protection against infection.

Diet and health

The food that children eat affects their health and development. Eating too much of the wrong foods can have serious consequences. For example, obesity in childhood has been linked to diabetes, heart disease and high blood pressure later in life (see *Childhood illness*).

Diet can also affect children's dental health. Foods with added sugar, such as fizzy drinks, are harmful to children's teeth and cause decay. Children should be given healthier alternatives such as fresh fruit and unsweetened juice.

Children's diet can also have an influence on their behaviour. Conditions such as Attention Deficit Hyperactivity Disorder (ADHD) have been linked to food additives such as colourings, artificial flavourings and preservatives (see *Challenging behaviour*).

Individual dietary needs

Children have different dietary needs for various reasons, including parental choice, religion, culture or specific medical conditions.

Some parents choose to be vegetarians (they do not eat meat or fish) or vegans (they do not eat any animal products, including eggs and cows' milk) and want their children to follow similar eating patterns.

Some religions and cultures have strict guidance about what kinds of food should be eaten. For example, Muslims do not eat pork and only eat halal meat (which has been killed according to Muslim law). Orthodox Jews do not eat pork and only eat food that is kosher (conforms to Jewish dietary laws).

Children with food intolerance may have difficulty digesting certain substances, leading to digestive symptoms such as diarrhoea. Some children experience food allergies when their immune system reacts abnormally to specific foods. Specialist food products are available for children with food allergies and intolerances.

Nutrition in early years settings

The Children's Food Trust outlines the government guidance for food and nutrition in early years settings in England. It highlights some of the ways that practitioners can support healthier eating habits for young children, including:

➤ Encouraging the enjoyment of food

➤ Offering interest and variety

➤ Developing independence through self-serving and making choices

➤ Supporting socialisation by eating together and developing table manners

➤ Involving children in food preparation by cooking, baking and growing their own food.

Case in point

Research has shown that children are more likely to develop healthy eating habits if they are involved in activities such as cooking, baking and growing their own food.

At Little Ducklings Nursery, the children enjoy simple activities such as chopping soft fruit and vegetables, such as bananas and cucumbers. They also like to mix the ingredients to bake pizzas, scones and muffins. All the children are involved in growing their own food in the nursery garden. At harvest time, the children delight in the food they have grown and this adds to their enjoyment of food and healthy eating.

Summary

Freshly prepared food with plenty of fruit and vegetables, wholegrain cereals, a source of protein (fish, meat, eggs, soya or cheese) and starchy food such as pasta provides young children with the essential nutrients they need for good health. Early years practitioners must understand the importance of a balanced diet, be aware of children's individual dietary needs and support children in developing lifelong, healthy eating habits.

Reference

The Children's Food Trust http://www.childrensfoodtrust.org.uk

Holistic development

Holistic development emphasises the importance of considering the development of the whole child. It refers to all areas of development (physical, cognitive, communication, emotional and social) and highlights the different ways in which these are linked. Early years practitioners must understand how the different areas of development can influence each other and be aware of the variation in children's developmental paths.

Principles of holistic development

Development is a continuous process, which begins at conception and continues throughout life into old age. It involves the development of skills and abilities, such as learning to walk and talk, and the maturing of body systems, such as bowel and bladder control. Development occurs in an orderly sequence, for example children will always learn to walk before they can run, climb or hop. However, the rate of development varies a great deal. Children should never be compared with each other as every child progresses in an individual way. The areas of development are all interconnected.

Areas of development

There are five main areas of child development (physical, cognitive, communication, emotional and social).

➤ Physical development relates to the development of physical skills (for example, balance and body coordination) and gross motor skills (for example, climbing, skipping and kicking a ball). It also includes the development of hand–eye coordination and fine motor skills (for example, threading beads, fastening buttons and using a pencil).

➤ Cognitive development relates to the development of children's thinking skills, including creativity, concentration and problem-solving. Communication development relates to the development of speech, language and non-verbal communication, including learning to talk and developing listening skills.

➤ Social and emotional development relates to the development of confidence, independence and self-esteem. It also includes how children learn to manage their feelings and behaviour and get along with others.

Interconnection of development

All areas of child development are linked in the following ways:

➤ Physical development affects children's opportunities to explore their environment and take risks, their ability to play with others and their independence. It therefore influences their social and emotional development and their behaviour.

➤ Cognitive and communication development affects all areas of children's learning, their ability to express themselves and play cooperatively. It therefore influences their social interaction and behaviour as well as their confidence and self-esteem.

➤ Social and emotional development affects how children develop relationships with others, build resilience and handle new situations. It has an impact on how children develop their understanding of acceptable behaviour and what is right and wrong.

Early years practitioners need to understand how all areas of child development are interconnected, in order to fully support children's individual developmental progress.

Case in point

Callum is 13 months old and is learning to walk. He needs to have the physical skills to move and coordinate his body, but he also needs confidence in his own abilities (emotional development) and an understanding of spatial awareness (cognitive development) to move around objects safely. Callum needs to trust his main carer to provide encouragement and a safe environment (social and emotional development) as he develops his skills in becoming more mobile.

Summary

All areas of child development are interlinked and influence each other in complex ways, through infancy to early childhood and beyond. It is important to view child development in a holistic way and to focus on the whole child rather than individual aspects of development.

Reference

STEARNS, J., SCHMIEDER, C. & YOUNG, K. (2013) *BTEC National Children's Play, Learning and Development*. London: HarperCollins Publishers.

Inclusive practice

Inclusion means ensuring that the needs of every child are recognised and catered for within the early years provision. Inclusion is concerned with attitudes as well as behaviour and practices. It is based on the rights of every child to have a safe, happy and fulfilled childhood regardless of their sex, religion or social origin (UNICEF, 1989). Inclusive practice acknowledges the individual needs of all children and recognises and celebrates diversity.

Promoting inclusive practice

Early years practitioners must promote inclusive practice and a positive attitude towards diversity. This responsibility is clearly outlined in legislation, including the Equality Act 2010, and involves meeting the needs of both boys and girls, children with special educational needs, children with disabilities and children from all social, cultural and religious backgrounds (see *Diversity*). Promoting inclusive practice in early years settings involves:

➤ Providing a safe and supportive environment for all children

➤ Providing a wide range of opportunities to support all children's learning and development

➤ Planning for each child's individual care

➤ Providing additional resources and a variety of teaching strategies, based on children's individual learning needs (differentiation)

➤ Working closely with parents and professionals from other agencies

➤ Using resources that represent diversity and challenge stereotypes

➤ Reflecting on attitudes towards diversity and confronting any incidence of discriminatory practice.

Benefits of inclusive practice

The benefits of inclusive practice are wide-reaching. For example:

➤ Celebrating the unique qualities and individual needs of every child is an important way for early years practitioners to combat discrimination and prejudice.

➤ Inclusive practice in early years settings helps children to feel valued and confident about their self-identity.

➤ It helps all children to have an equal chance to learn and develop and to participate fully in all activities.

➤ Inclusive practice helps children understand that their individual needs will be recognised and met. This supports them to feel safe and have a sense of belonging in the setting.

➤ The way in which young children experience attitudes towards gender, ethnicity, culture and social background has an impact on the expectations they develop about their future and can influence their long-term achievement and success.

Case in point

Woodlands Nursery demonstrates inclusive practice. The practitioners use materials that children can access through sight, touch, sound and smell, adaptive technology and digital devices according to their individual needs. Wall displays show families from different ethnic groups. There are books in a variety of community languages, role-play materials and dressing-up clothes from a range of different countries and cultures, and dolls and puppets representing different genders and disabilities. The children are learning *Twinkle, Twinkle, Little Star* in English, Polish and with Makaton signs.

Andrew, who uses a wheelchair, can access activities and play experiences using his specialist aids and equipment. Different activities are planned to enrich Andrew's learning. The staff work closely with other professionals to support the individual needs of children in the setting. This includes a speech and language therapist and the traveller education service coordinated by the setting's Special Educational Needs Coordinator (SENCo).

Summary

Inclusive practice does not mean treating everyone the same but ensuring that all children have the same opportunities to make progress according to their needs. It means seeing each child as an individual with unique qualities and particular needs, and celebrating diversity and difference. Early years practitioners should support the learning and development of each child in ways that are appropriate to their abilities, interests and needs.

References

Department for Education (2001) *Special Educational Needs Code of Practice.* Cm 8027. http://www.education.gov.uk

Department for Education (2011) *Support and Aspiration: A New Approach to Special Educational Needs and Disability. Cm 8027.* http://www.education.gov.uk

Equality Act 2010 (c. 15). London: The Stationery Office. http://www. legislation.gov.uk

UNICEF (UK) (1989) *United Nations Convention on the Rights of the Child.* http://www.unicef.org.uk

Infant feeding

Infant feeding refers to the different feeding methods required for infants. During the first six months of life, the nutritional needs of a baby can be completely satisfied by breast milk or infant formula milk. From six months, the process of weaning will gradually introduce the baby to solid food. Feeding routines in infancy help to establish eating patterns throughout childhood and create a foundation for a healthy lifestyle.

Breast-feeding

The World Health Organization (WHO) recommends that babies are exclusively breast-fed for the first six months of life. Breast milk is nutritionally balanced for newborn babies and is easier to digest. Breast-feeding helps to promote attachment between the mother and baby and carries less risk of infectious conditions, such as gastroenteritis. Breast-fed babies are less likely to develop allergies or become obese in later childhood.

The first milk to be produced by the breasts is called colostrum. This substance is very high in calories and also contains antibodies from the mother which protect the baby from infection.

Bottle-feeding

Bottle-feeding uses formula milk, which is specially modified cows' milk designed for babies. Ordinary cows' milk contains too much salt (sodium) for babies and high levels of a protein called casein, which is difficult for babies to digest. Formula milk feeds should always be prepared according to the instructions and all feeding equipment should be thoroughly cleaned and sterilised (see *Cross-infection*). One advantage of bottle-feeding is that the father, partner or other people can also feed the baby.

Weaning

Weaning is the process of introducing solid food into a baby's diet. The Department of Health recommends that the weaning process is started at six months. Starting solid food too early can be harmful for babies and can lead to the baby developing some allergies.

Solid food should be introduced gradually. Very small amounts of puréed food should be offered to the baby using a sterilised plastic teaspoon. A wider variety of foods can be introduced as the baby gets used to chewing. However, the Department of Health recommends avoiding certain foods during the weaning process, for example:

➤ raw eggs (to minimise the risk of salmonella)

➤ salt (which can damage the baby's kidneys)

➤ sugar (to prevent tooth decay)

➤ honey (can produce toxins leading to the condition infant botulism)

➤ low-fat foods (fat is an important source of calories and some vitamins for babies).

Babies can gradually be given the same food as the rest of the family and will enjoy feeding themselves with a spoon or with their fingers.

Mealtime routines

Feeding time is always special whether a baby is breast- or bottle-fed. The parent and baby can enjoy being close and it is important for developing the attachment relationship.

Once weaning is established, it is important to encourage a baby to be part of the family at mealtimes. A baby can sit in a highchair at the family table and enjoy being included.

At mealtimes babies learn self-help and social skills, such as being part of a group, developing independence and learning to communicate their needs.

Summary

Whether babies are breast- or bottle-fed, this early stage of infant feeding helps to establish a close attachment between the parent and baby. The process of weaning introduces the baby to a wider variety of foods and provides the basis for developing healthy eating in later life.

References

Department of Health https://www.gov.uk/government/organisations/department-of-health

World Health Organization http://www.who.int/nutrition/topics/infantfeeding/en/

Inspection

Inspection is a rigorous process of regular checks that are carried out in all settings that provide early education, to assess the quality and standards for the welfare, learning and development of the children.

The inspection process

The inspection process varies between the four countries of the UK, but the main principles are the same. The different inspectorates are:

➤ The Office for Standards in Education, Children's Services and Skills (Ofsted) in England

➤ Education Scotland

➤ Her Majesty's Inspectorate for Education and Training in Wales (Estyn)

➤ The Education and Training Inspectorate (ETI) in Northern Ireland.

Inspectors usually visit the setting unannounced and spend time observing staff and children, and speaking with parents and carers. To reach an overall judgement, inspectors ask themselves, 'What difference is this provider making to the learning, development and progress of children in their care?' (Ofsted, 2013). The inspection process in England includes judgements in the following categories:

➤ the overall effectiveness of the early years provision

➤ the effectiveness of leadership and management of the early years provision

➤ the quality of the provision in the Early Years Foundation Stage

➤ outcomes for children in the Early Years Foundation Stage.

Inspectors collect first-hand evidence based on the practice they observe in the setting, and use this information to produce their inspection report. These reports are publicly available (usually on the inspectorate's website) and must be made available for parents (see *Parents as partners*). In England, inspections are carried out on all newly registered settings and at least every three to four years after that.

The inspection report

There are variations in the format of inspection reports, but in general, the report summarises the overall effectiveness of the early years provision and the steps that need to be taken to improve provision further. In England, the Ofsted inspection report summarises the quality and standards of the provision and outcomes for children in the Early Years Foundation Stage. Inspectors give providers one of four grades:

➤ Outstanding

➤ Good

➤ Requires improvement

➤ Inadequate.

Settings that are judged 'inadequate' will generally be given a notice to improve within a specific time frame. Inspection reports enable parents to make informed decisions when choosing an early years setting and help practitioners to create action plans to develop the provision and improve quality in the setting.

The government report *More Great Childcare* (DfE, 2013) proposes giving more power to Ofsted inspections and conducting more frequent inspections for weaker childcare providers.

Case in point

Here is an example extract from an inspection report for a setting graded 'outstanding':

'Children are cared for within four rooms and have continuous access to a secure outdoor play area. The nursery supports children who speak English as an additional language, practitioners know the children's individual backgrounds, and they organise interesting activities to help them learn about diversity.

The environment is bright and welcoming, with a very spacious and well-equipped outdoor area. There are some good-quality play materials to support children's enjoyment and learning.

Staff form positive and friendly relationships with parents and carers. They keep them informed about the children's day and have effective systems to involve parents in children's learning.

There is a well-qualified staff team who all demonstrate secure knowledge of the Early Years Foundation Stage framework. Learning journals include observations of children's development, and the next steps in their learning are consistently identified.

Children behave well in the setting because the staff set appropriate boundaries and help children to learn the difference between right and wrong.'

It is unlikely that this inspection report would include any significant actions. Under the current system, the next inspection would not be scheduled for at least three years.

Summary

The inspection of early years education helps to ensure the provision of high quality care for children's learning and development. Inspection reports provide an invaluable resource for parents and a constructive means for practitioners to continually improve the quality of care they provide.

References

Department for Education (2013) *More Great Childcare: Raising Quality and Giving Parents More Choice*. http://www.education.gov.uk

Education Scotland http://www.educationscotland.gov.uk

Estyn (Wales) http://www.estyn.gov.uk

Eti (Northern Ireland) http://www.etini.gov.uk

Ofsted http://www.ofsted.gov.uk

Key person

The key person is a named member of staff who has a special responsibility for the care of specific children in the setting. The key person will ensure that each child's care is tailored to meet their individual needs, help children become familiar with the setting and build a relationship with their parents. It is a requirement of the Statutory Framework for the Early Years Foundation Stage (EYFS) that all children in registered settings have a key person.

The role of a key person

The role of a key person varies slightly in different early years settings. For example, in a nursery setting, the key person is usually responsible for a small group of key children, observing and monitoring their development and communicating with their parents. With babies, this will usually involve responsibility for individual personal care, such as nappy changing and feeding.

The key person system in early years settings is based on the principles of attachment theory (see *Attachment*). The key person responds sensitively to the child's demands and regularly engages in playful interactions. The child prefers to be with their key person and will often refuse to go to other practitioners in the setting. The key person has a powerful impact on all areas of a child's wellbeing, learning and development.

Communicating with parents

Parents must know that their child will be happy and safe in an early years setting, and being able to trust a special person to be responsible for this means that they will have peace of mind and confidence in the setting.

The key person needs to know about anything that may affect the child during their time at the setting, for example a change in routine or events in the family, such as the arrival of a new baby. This helps the key person to be aware of and respond to changes in the child's behaviour or individual needs.

In many early years settings, the key person is responsible for actively involving parents in monitoring the child's progress, through sharing observations and developmental records and planning relevant play experiences. Communication between parents and the key person is therefore an important two-way process. This acknowledges parents' unique knowledge about their own children and supports the practice of working in partnership (see *Parents as partners*).

Case in point

Suri is four years old and has recently started at Apple Tree Nursery. Emma is Suri's key person. She is starting to get to know Suri and her family. Emma always makes time to speak with Suri's mother when she drops Suri off and picks her up. She has found out that Suri enjoys music and dancing and that she has a new baby brother. Emma spends some special time with Suri every morning and has been sharing some books with her about new babies. She makes sure that Suri has the opportunity every day to dance to a variety of music from different cultures, and she provides ribbons and costumes for Suri to create imaginative dance routines.

Emma regularly observes Suri and shares her observations with Suri's mother. In this way, Emma is meeting Suri's individual needs and developing a special relationship with both Suri and her family.

Summary

A strong attachment relationship with a key person in the setting is very important for a child's personal, emotional and social development. It provides the child with a secure base, which helps them to feel cherished and safe while they are away from home. The key person has an extremely important role in an early years setting, with a responsibility for supporting children's learning and development and acting as the main point of contact with children's parents.

References

Department for Education (2012) *Statutory Framework for the Early Years Foundation Stage.* http://www.education.gov.uk

ELFER, P., GOLDSCHMIED, E. & SELLECK, D. (2011) *Key Persons in the Early Years: Building Relationships for Quality Provision in Early Years Settings and Primary Schools.* London: Routledge.

Learning through play

When engaged in play, children are learning through hands-on experience, exploring, experimenting and following their own interests. Play helps young children to become competent learners who can make connections and transform ideas.

Supporting children's learning through play

To effectively promote children's learning through play, practitioners should offer a stimulating, safe environment for learning with a range of appropriate resources, both inside and outside the setting. Simple materials, for example sand and water, a selection of tubing, an assortment of fabric or large cardboard boxes can inspire children's imaginations (see *Play resources*). Children explore through their play and experiment with new ideas as they find out what things do.

Early years practitioners can support children's learning through play by:

➤ observing children and providing appropriate intervention

➤ providing opportunities and resources for hands-on exploration

➤ helping children to build on what they can do, and to make connections in their developing knowledge and understanding

➤ giving children choices and helping them to make decisions.

Child-initiated play

Research for the Effective Provision of Pre-school Education (EPPE) project has confirmed the importance of play in early learning. The project concluded that early years settings should offer a balance of adult-directed activities and child-initiated play, which promotes children's learning.

Child-initiated play is characterised by free-flow play activities, which are principally decided, motivated and controlled by the child. However, good learning opportunities will evolve best when adults intervene effectively and sensitively in children's play to take their ideas further, when required. The Early Years Foundation Stage (EYFS) states that 'when children engage in free-flow play, they are able to learn at their highest level' (DfE, 2012).

Professor Tina Bruce suggests that free-flow play is coordinated, moves fluidly from one scenario to the next and makes young children feel powerful and contented.

Case in point

Tom, aged four years, often plays outside at the nursery and has been investigating different lengths of drainpipe placed in the 'Builder's Yard'. Tom's key person, Annie, has observed him pouring water into the top of a drainpipe and watching it come out at the bottom. Tom fetches a small watering can he has filled from the outside tap. "Watch," he says, as the water runs down the pipe onto the ground. "It's coming out fast." Tom rearranges the pipe so that it touches the drain. He refills the watering can and repeats the pouring action. Tom watches and says, "It comes down the pipe and goes in the hole, then it's gone!"

"I wonder where it's gone?" says Annie. "How could you collect the water?"

Tom is clearly learning through his play. He is showing curiosity about why things happen and how things work, using hands-on play experiences to investigate his ideas and solve problems. Annie is supporting Tom's play through sensitive intervention, by providing materials, asking open-ended questions and encouraging him to verbalise his ideas and experience (see *Creative, critical thinking*).

Summary

In their play, children notice, practise, experiment with ideas and make adaptations as their understanding grows. This gives children the opportunity to investigate, ask questions, experiment and solve problems. Child-initiated play helps children to make decisions, try out different solutions and achieve a new understanding about the world around them. Early years practitioners need to nurture this process so that children's sense of wonder and excitement is maintained at the same time as their learning is being supported and developed.

References

BRUCE, T. (2011) *Learning Through Play: For Babies, Toddlers and Young Children*. 2nd Ed. London: Hodder Education.

Department for Education (2012) *Statutory Framework for the Early Years Foundation Stage*. http://www.education.gov.uk

Multi-agency working

'Multi-agency working' and 'integrated working' are terms used to describe the way that services work together in different ways to meet the needs of children and their families. This way of working has been shown to be an effective way of addressing the wide range of risk factors that contribute to poorer outcomes for children and their families.

Multi-agency working

Multi-agency working refers to different agencies working together to provide services that meet the needs of children and their families, for example when practitioners from health, education and social care departments work together to provide support for a family and their child with Down's syndrome.

Integrated working

Integrated working refers to different services joining together, usually in the same building, to offer more effective care for children and families, for example in a children's centre, parents may be able to seek advice from a health visitor, attend a play session with their toddler and access a training programme to improve their own education or employment prospects.

The benefits of working together

When professionals work together to provide services for children and families, each practitioner brings their own specialist skills, expertise and insight to provide the best quality care and support. The benefits of this include:

➤ Early identification of children's needs

➤ Quicker access to services and early intervention

➤ Better support for parents

➤ Better quality services.

Barriers to effective partnership working

For multi-agency and integrated working to operate effectively, all the professionals involved must respect each other. Some of the barriers to effective partnership working include:

➤ Roles not clearly defined

➤ Poor communication or lack of information sharing between partners

➤ Lack of coordination between different service providers

➤ Inaccurate or inconsistent record keeping

➤ Ineffective policies and procedures

➤ Lack of evaluation and no review process of service provision.

The Common Assessment Framework (CAF)

The Common Assessment Framework (CAF) was introduced in England in 2005 and is a standardised framework for assessing the needs of children and their families. It enables practitioners across all agencies to communicate and work more effectively together and its main aim is to help practitioners make a holistic assessment of children's additional needs, highlight the strengths and needs of the child and family and identify what support is needed (see *Early intervention*). The CAF reduces duplication of assessment, encourages a shared language across agencies and improves referrals between agencies. The main sections of the CAF include summaries of:

➤ the child's development: their health and progress in learning

➤ parents and carers: how well parents are able to support their child's development

➤ family and environmental: the impact of wider family and environmental elements, such as housing.

Case in point

Emma is four years old and her childminder brings her to the Alphabet Nursery every morning. Beth is Emma's key person at the nursery and she has noticed that Emma can sometimes be very aggressive with other children. Beth mentioned this to Emma's childminder who said that Emma's mother has just had a new baby and had to spend some time in hospital. Beth discussed the situation with her manager who suggested contacting a family support worker and a referral to Emma's health visitor. Beth suggests this to the childminder and together they work out a plan with Emma's mother.

Summary

Multi-agency working and integrated working bring together practitioners from different sectors and professions to provide an integrated way of working to support children and families. This ensures that children have the right professionals to support them, and is likely to include people from backgrounds such as social work, health, education and early years who will deliver a coordinated package of support that is centred on the child.

Reference

Department for Education (2007) *Multi-agency Working: Fact Sheet.* http://www.education.gov.uk

Nature and nurture

The nature–nurture debate has been discussed by theorists and practitioners for many decades. Some people believe that biological factors inherited from parents (nature) have a more powerful influence on children's development, while others believe that it is the quality of a child's environment (nurture) that is the most important factor. Research clearly shows that both are important in determining a child's future.

The influence of nature

Theorists who support the idea that nature is the more powerful influence are known as nativists. They believe that individual differences are due to each child's unique genetic code. Nativists also argue that these biological factors influence behaviours, such as attachment in infancy, language acquisition and even cognitive development as a whole. John Bowlby and Noam Chomsky both supported this view (see *Theories*).

Numerous studies have been conducted involving identical twins, separated at birth and raised apart in completely different circumstances. These studies discovered that identical twins had widespread similarities in personality, career choice and even mannerisms in later life, and demonstrated the powerful influence of genes (nature).

The influence of nurture

Theorists who support the idea that nurture is the more powerful influence are known as environmentalists (or empiricists). They believe that at birth, a child's mind is a blank slate, which gradually develops as a result of experience. Environmentalists believe that children's characteristics and behavioural differences are the result of learning through stimulation, encouragement and opportunities. Albert Bandura and Burrhus Frederic Skinner both supported this view (see *Theories*).

Interactions between nature and nurture

Research is increasingly showing that the influence of nature and nurture cannot be separated as easily as previously thought. There is a strong relationship between the environment we live in and the genes in our cells, so identifying the influence of each on our development is becoming more difficult.

Implications for early years practice

Studies including the Effective Provision of Pre-school Education (EPPE) have found that good quality pre-school experience can significantly enhance children's development. This kind of research supports the influence of environmental factors on children's learning and development (nurture). Some of the factors which have the most significant impact include:

➤ early years practitioners with higher-level qualifications

➤ early years settings where educational and social development are seen as equally important

➤ the quality of adult–child interactions

➤ practitioners' knowledge and understanding of the early years curriculum.

Case in point

Cindy, aged four years, is about to start in Reception class. She is able to read simple picture books and write her own name. She has an extensive and varied vocabulary and knows several songs and rhymes by heart.

Malik is also four years old and starting in Reception class. He struggles to hold a pencil accurately and has a very short attention span. He has a limited vocabulary and has difficulty in managing his behaviour and playing cooperatively with other children.

It could be argued that both nature and nurture have influenced the development of Malik and Cindy. All children are different and it is very important for early years practitioners to be aware of all the different factors that can affect children's learning and development.

Summary

Children's development is influenced by the genes they inherit from their parents and the environment in which they are brought up. These two factors are sometimes referred to as nature (genes) and nurture (environmental influences). The nature–nurture debate is ongoing. A child's development is likely to depend on the genes they inherit, but also the level of stimulation, encouragement and opportunities they have to reach their potential.

Reference

Institute of Education, University of London, Effective Provision of Pre-school Education (EPPE) project. http://www.ioe.ac.uk

Observation

The process of observation (watching and listening) forms the foundation of professional early years practice. Observing children's play, development and behaviour helps practitioners to identify children's interests and assess their individual needs. This will help them to plan meaningful activities to support children's early learning.

The observation, assessment and planning cycle

Observation describes the process of watching and listening to children. Assessment involves analysing those observations and pulling together the information to make a judgement about the child's progress. This enables practitioners to plan activities and experiences that support children's learning and development. Observation, assessment and planning all feed into one another and this is often represented as a cycle.

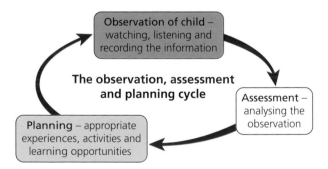

The observation, assessment and planning cycle

Observation

Observation is one of the most important aspects of day-to-day professional practice when working with children of all ages. It enables practitioners to see each child as an individual and to discover their specific needs and interests by carefully looking, listening and then recording information. In early years settings, observations of children are conducted on both a formal (planned) and informal (spontaneous) basis and should include information from parents or carers. Observation helps practitioners to monitor a child's developmental progress and to keep the child at the centre of their practice.

Methods of recording observations include:

➤ Written narrative: providing a full, written report

➤ Time sample: observing at regular intervals for a set period of time

➤ Event sample: focusing on a specific aspect of development or behaviour

➤ Checklist: a structured method for monitoring children's developmental progress

➤ Digital recordings (visual and audio): recording children's communication or providing visual evidence of children's play or development

➤ Target child: focusing on a specific aspect of learning or development of an individual child

➤ Learning journey: a combination of photographs, narrative and information from parents.

Modern methods are generally less formal than this and planning originates more from spontaneous observations and reflections with the children.

Assessment

Assessment is the process of analysing and reviewing what has been observed about children's development and learning.

Formative assessment is based on regular, everyday observation and guides day-to-day planning in early years settings. Summative assessment is a summary of all the formative assessment carried out over a long period and can be used to make statements about the child's progress.

The two-year-old check and the EYFS Profile (see *EYFS*) are examples of summative assessments and can be found in the Statutory Framework for the Early Years Foundation Stage (DfE, 2012).

Planning

Effective planning enables early years practitioners to support children's learning and development in both the long and short term.

➤ Short-term planning focuses on the day-to-day provision in the setting and is based on observation of children's individual needs and interests. This will include the resources required as well as any specific health and safety considerations relevant to the children's stage of development.

➤ Medium-term planning usually outlines the overall programme in the setting for around two to six weeks at a time, including appropriate experiences and activities for the children (indoors and outdoors), daily routines and the main resources for areas of continuous provision, such as the role-play area or sand and water play areas.

➤ Long-term planning provides a structure which helps practitioners to meet the learning and development needs of all the children in the setting. In England, this is directed by the Statutory Framework for the Early Years Foundation Stage (EYFS), which helps practitioners to support children's play, learning and development (see *EYFS*).

Nowadays, most modern planning is short term, as medium- and long-term planning do not respond easily to children's immediate interests. However, practitioners need to ensure that their planning meets the overall long-term goals of the EYFS for children's learning and development.

Case in point

Sophie is 10 months old and is sitting alongside a treasure basket exploring the contents. The treasure basket is filled with a range of natural materials, including large pine cones, large shells, soft brushes, shiny objects and other natural materials.

Jess is Sophie's key person and observes the following:

Sophie sits sturdily and reaches for objects using both hands independently. She spends a long time exploring a shiny spoon, puts it in her mouth, looks at it intently and waves it around. Sophie seems to enjoy exploring the mirror, she looks at her reflection, licks the mirror and laughs at Jess. Sophie is fully engaged with the treasure basket for 10 minutes.

Jess will record her observation as part of Sophie's learning journey. She will use this information to plan the next steps for Sophie's learning and development, and will provide a different variety of shiny materials and other objects for Sophie to explore.

Jess will continue to observe Sophie's play and share her observations with Sophie's parents. She will use this information to monitor Sophie's progress within the EYFS.

Summary

Observation, assessment and planning form the basis of everyday work in early years settings.

Observation enables practitioners to form a clear picture of each child in order to meet their individual needs and interests.

Assessment provides guidance for analysing the information from observations and making judgements about children's learning and development.

Planning helps practitioners to provide appropriate experiences and activities for children within a structure which supports learning and development and satisfies the requirements of the relevant framework.

References

Department for Education (2012) *Statutory Framework for the Early Years Foundation Stage.* http://www.education.gov.uk

Foundation Years http://www.foundationyears.org.uk

Outdoor learning

Learning outdoors (outside) provides children with different experiences to enhance their learning and development. It is widely recognised that spending time outdoors is important for children's health and development.

The importance of outdoor learning

A growing interest in digital technology, coupled with an increase in fears about children's safety, has contributed to a decrease in children's outdoor play.

Learning outdoors is beneficial to children as it:

➤ supports the development of healthy, active lifestyles and offers children the opportunity for physical activity, freedom and movement

➤ provides safe and supervised opportunities for children to experience new challenges, assess risk and develop the skills to manage difficult situations

➤ provides rich opportunities for imagination and resourcefulness and supports children's developing creativity and problem-solving skills

➤ provides opportunities for children to express their feelings, develop confidence in new situations and become more independent (see *Learning through play*).

Supporting learning and development outdoors

Personal, social and emotional development
Activities involving growing and taking care of living things provide ways for children to develop care and concern for the environment. Social relationships can be developed as children share problems, discuss solutions and negotiate resolution.

The outdoors can provide a safe place for children to explore new challenges and learn to manage risks, increasing their confidence and self-esteem (see *Risk assessment*).

Communication and language

Children can hear and respond to a wide range of sounds and develop their listening skills as they recognise different noises in the outdoor environment. They are stimulated by new vocabulary, conversation and questioning, which support their communication and language for learning (see *Communication*).

Physical development

Children can be much more physically active outdoors, with opportunities to develop body coordination, balance and stamina. Children can develop their fine motor skills and dexterity through the control of gardening tools or small play equipment.

Playing outdoors supports children's awareness of personal health and safety, for example through hand-washing routines after digging.

Mathematical development

Children can explore and develop an understanding of mathematical language and concepts, such as shape, space and measure, for example filling containers with soil or stones, creating leaf patterns or observing how plants have grown. Natural materials, such as twigs and cones, can be counted, sorted and classified according to size or shape.

Understanding the world

Children can explore different materials, for example touching plants, smelling flowers or watching the movements of insects. The cycle of plant growth and seasonal changes help children to understand the concept of time, and the outdoors provides an environment for practical investigation, for example exploring spiders' webs. Children can use digital technology outdoors to record sounds or photograph interesting objects.

Literacy

The outdoors provides a rich environment for creating stories, using natural props to enhance children's imagination. It is also an ideal setting for sharing books and poetry or enacting songs and rhymes. Children can make marks in wet sand or damp soil, or with large, chunky chalks, helping to develop control of the small muscles needed for successful handwriting.

Expressive arts and design

Children can explore using all their senses and express their ideas and feelings through music, dance, art and role-play. They can explore natural materials in two and three dimensions and represent their ideas using techniques such as leaf printing.

Summary

Outdoor learning complements indoor learning in early years settings and is equally important. It encompasses all that children do, see, hear or feel in the outdoor environment, including naturally occurring opportunities linked to the seasons, weather and nature. Effective early years practice outdoors involves providing opportunities for children to be energetic, adventurous and messy, but also to hide, relax and reflect.

References

Learning Through Landscapes http://www.ltl.org.uk

OUVRY, M. (2005) *Going Out to Play and Learn*. British Association for Early Childhood Education. http://www.early-education.org.uk

PALMER, S. (2007) *Toxic Childhood: How the Modern World is Damaging Our Children and What We Can Do About It*. London: Orion Books.

Parents as partners

Practitioners can develop important relationships with the parents of the children they care for. Research has shown that 'young children achieve more and are happier when early years educators work together with parents' (Athey, 2007). Quality relationships support effective communication between the setting and the home, which leads to an increase in knowledge about individual children. Good communication helps parents and staff to work together to provide positive learning experiences.

Working in partnership

'Parents are a child's first and most enduring educators' (Parents, Early Years and Learning) and there is overwhelming evidence that children benefit when early years educators and parents work together. Children feel more confident about themselves and their learning when parents and practitioners work together in an atmosphere of mutual respect.

The first contact parents have with practitioners sets the tone for the future. Parents should be greeted warmly and made to feel welcome in the setting. Parents from different ethnic groups or who do not speak English as their first language may feel particularly uneasy, and practitioners must appreciate parents' different backgrounds, values and beliefs (see *Inclusive practice*).

All parents approach the job of parenting in different ways and early years practitioners need to understand and accept the wide variety of family structures and parenting styles (see *Family structures*). Practitioners must be clear about their professional responsibilities; there is a difference between being a friendly professional and a parent's friend. Practitioners must always put the needs of the child first and respond appropriately.

Relationships with parents must be built on firm foundations and this can be achieved by:

➤ recognising that parents are their child's first educators

➤ sharing information and observations with parents about children's development in a respectful way

➤ conducting home visits and gathering information from the home

➤ using a key person system in the setting

➤ organising daily times for communication and special open evenings

➤ respecting all parents' beliefs and cultures, whether or not they coincide with your own.

Communication

The Statutory Framework for the Early Years Foundation Stage (see *EYFS*) states that the following information must be made available to parents:

➤ How the EYFS is being delivered in the setting (including the range and type of activities, daily routines and how parents and carers can share learning at home)

➤ How the setting supports children with special educational needs and disabilities

➤ Food and drinks provided for children

➤ Details of policies and procedures in the setting

➤ Staffing information (including the name of their child's key person).

All settings communicate with parents in different ways, including phone calls, texts, letters, email, the internet, leaflets, posters, pictures and notice boards. It is important that all communication with parents is inclusive, using plain English (with translation where appropriate), and conveys information clearly (see *Recording and reporting*).

Case in point

The staff team at Little Acorns Nursery work hard to develop partnerships with parents. They have an 'open door' policy and welcome parents into the setting at any time. They always make time to talk with parents and listen to their concerns and provide a parents room for private discussions or social meetings. They are aware of parents whose first language is not English and try to provide information in a variety of community languages. Each member of staff keeps parents informed about their child's progress and shares observation and developmental records on a regular basis.

The staff organise regular coffee mornings and parent days and encourage parents to help out with special events at the nursery such as sport and activity days. The staff also utilise the specific expertise of individual parents in the community and have recently invited different parents to share an Indian dancing session and a Chinese cookery session with the children.

Summary

The outcomes for children are better when practitioners and parents work closely together. All parents can enhance their child's development and learning and have a right to play a central role in making decisions about their child's care and education. Good quality relationships between parents, practitioners and children are fundamental, and these relationships need to be built on respect, based on the principles of equality and diversity.

References

ATHEY, C. (2007) *Extending Thought in Young Children: A Parent–Teacher Partnership.* London: Paul Chapman Publishing.

Parents, Early Years and Learning (PEAL) http://www.peal.org.uk

Pen Green Centre http://www.pengreen.org

Play resources

Play resources are anything that children can use in their play activities. In early years settings, the most valuable resource in any play activity is usually the practitioner. However, certain well-chosen resources can enhance children's play experiences and support their learning and development. All play resources provided for children should be safe, stimulating and adaptable for use both indoors and outside of the setting.

Choosing play resources

There is a vast range of play resources available for babies and children of all ages. Simple play materials, such as cardboard boxes and household objects, can offer opportunities for creative play. Equally, many children enjoy computers and electronic toys, and these can form an important part of their learning. Practitioners should provide a balance of resources.

All play resources should be suitable for the child's age and stage of development. They should be adaptable and fully accessible for children with special educational needs (see *SEN*).

Many shop-bought plastic resources have a limited or fixed play value. The best resources to extend children's creativity and develop their problem-solving skills are open-ended resources that can be used for a variety of types of play, for example natural resources that are free and can be collected by the children themselves, such as stones, twigs, fir cones and shells.

Treasure baskets

From birth, children learn through experiences in their everyday environment. The opportunity for sensory exploration is a very important part of early learning. As soon as babies can sit comfortably and handle objects, they can be given a treasure basket to play with.

A treasure basket is a collection of natural objects (such as fir cones, cotton reels, tin lids, pebbles and scented bags) in a sturdy, low-sided basket. The purpose of treasure basket play is to offer maximum interest through exploration using the five senses. Babies gain rich sensory experiences through mouthing and handling objects, and show great curiosity and high levels of concentration.

Heuristic play

The term 'heuristic' comes from the Greek *eurisko*, which means to discover or gain an understanding. Heuristic play naturally follows on from treasure baskets, when babies become mobile toddlers. It is the early stage of exploratory play in which children are absorbed by filling and emptying, and using objects and containers of all kinds.

In heuristic play, children become absorbed in pursuing their own exploration with intense concentration and developing creative, critical thinking (see *Creative, critical thinking*).

Materials should be provided in large quantities, all in separate bags, which can then be easily put away when not in use, for example woollen pom-poms, tins of various sizes, wooden curtain rings, metal rings or bracelets and cardboard cylinders.

The adult is an observer, facilitating the session by providing the materials and being quietly attentive to the children's play.

Other play resources

A wide variety of resources can be provided to support children's play, learning and development in the following areas (see *Learning through play*):

Physical play

Resources for physical play should encourage children to be active, develop their physical skills and challenge them to take risks. Climbing frames, wheeled toys, hoops, bats and balls, obstacle courses, parachute games, planks, crates and large boxes all support children's active play and gross motor development.

Imaginative play

Resources for imaginative play should encourage children to take on different roles, engage in 'let's pretend' games and express their feelings. Dressing-up clothes, blankets, lengths of fabric, large cardboard boxes and small world toys all provide opportunities for children to use their imagination and express themselves.

Creative play

Resources for creative play should encourage children to express their ideas in a variety of different ways. Paint, materials for mark-making, drawing, printing and modelling, musical instruments and ribbons for dancing all provide resources for children to be creative and represent their ideas.

Sensory play

Resources for sensory play should encourage children to use all of their senses to experience, explore and experiment. Sand, water, dough, cornflour, shaving foam, cooked pasta, wood shavings, compost, bark chippings, pebbles, sticks, mud and straw all provide a variety of experiences for sensory play both inside and outdoors.

Construction play

Resources for construction play should encourage children to explore ideas and experiment with how things work. Construction sets, wooden blocks, large-scale modelling materials (such as cardboard boxes, plastic tubing, metal pipes), recycled materials and woodworking tools all support the development of children's spatial awareness and problem-solving skills (see *Creative, critical thinking*).

Summary

Carefully selected play resources are an important element of early years provision. Skilled practitioners observe children's play, provide play resources to complement children's individual interests, inspire creativity and support learning and development.

References

BRUCE, T. (2004) *Developing Learning in Early Childhood*. London: Hodder & Stoughton.

GOLDSCHMIED, E. (1987*) Infants at Work*. London: Routledge.

Policies and procedures

A policy is a collectively agreed statement of beliefs, which is usually presented as a document that informs procedures. A procedure is a course of action to be taken in particular circumstances. Policies and procedures in early years settings should be regularly reviewed and changes made, where necessary, in consultation with the staff team and parents.

Policy requirements

To fulfil the requirements of inspection, early years settings must have certain policies in place (see *Inspection*).
In England, this is also a requirement of the Statutory Framework for the Early Years Foundation Stage (EYFS).

Policies required by Ofsted for inspection purposes include:

➤ Special Educational Needs

➤ Safeguarding Children

➤ Behaviour Management

➤ Confidentiality

➤ Working in Partnership with Parents and Carers

➤ Accidents and Emergencies

➤ Equality of Opportunity and Inclusion.

Many settings also have policies for situations such as the admission of children, healthy eating and the provision of intimate care (like nappy changing and toileting). All policy documents should be available for the whole staff team and parents to read. Staff should sign to say they have read, agree with and will abide by each policy and procedure.

Requirements for procedures

Equally, there are specific requirements for procedures within early years settings. These should clearly set out the procedure to be followed in certain situations, for example:

➤ If an allegation of child abuse is made against a member of staff

➤ In the event of a parent and/or carer failing to collect a child

➤ In the event of a child going missing from the setting

➤ In dealing with concerns and complaints from parents.

Many settings also have established procedures for functions such as conducting child observations, snack time, risk assessments and other daily routines.

Case in point

Here is an example of an Equal Opportunities and Inclusion Policy for an early years setting:

"This setting believes that equality of opportunity for all those in our care is vital. All our policies, procedures and practices reflect the rights of all children and adults, including those with special educational needs or disabilities, all ethnic and cultural groups and those with English as an additional language. This setting has a zero tolerance attitude towards any form of discrimination and will challenge any inappropriate attitudes and practices.

The aims of our policy:

➤ To ensure the individual care and learning needs of all children are met.

➤ To ensure all children are able to develop in a caring and considerate environment where everyone is valued for their contribution to nursery life.

➤ To work in partnership with parents and carers who are fully involved in all decisions that affect their children's care and education.

➤ To work with agencies and other care providers in a professional and open manner to enable individual needs to be met in a timely and purposeful way.

➤ To provide the highest possible quality support and inclusive care and education for children with SEN or other additional needs.

➤ To develop children's sense of identity and raise their self-esteem by creating an environment which recognises them as individuals."

Summary

Policies and procedures establish a firm foundation in early years settings. Policies ensure that settings comply with legal obligations and reflect the general ethos and way of working. Procedures help staff to maintain standards of care and continue to improve the quality of provision in the setting.

Reference

Department for Education (2012) *Statutory Framework for the Early Years Foundation Stage*. http://www.education.gov.uk

Positive behaviour

Positive behaviour is often referred to as acceptable or appropriate behaviour which conforms to accepted values and beliefs. It is defined as being helpful and constructive.

Expectations for behaviour

Many different factors influence our understanding of positive behaviour, including family background and culture. Children need help in developing positive behaviour patterns and practitioners have an important responsibility to act as role models in early years settings.

Young children must learn how to behave appropriately, just as they learn to walk and talk, and they need adult help to do this.

Early years practitioners need to have a sound understanding of holistic child development and realistic expectations about children's capabilities. For example, it would be unrealistic to expect toddlers to share their toys or understand the danger of climbing onto a high windowsill.

The importance of rules and boundaries

In early years settings, policies and procedures provide a framework for appropriate behaviour to ensure that everyone knows the rules and is treated fairly (see *Policies and procedures*). Rules and boundaries help children to know what is expected of them and feel secure. One of the most successful ways of developing behaviour policies is to include children in creating the rules and ensuring that the rules are subsequently enforced consistently. Even quite young children can be encouraged to think about how they should behave and how they would like others to behave towards them.

Positive reinforcement

One of the most effective ways to support positive behaviour in children is to focus on the positive rather than the negative. Telling children what they should do, rather than what they shouldn't do, helps children develop appropriate behaviour patterns, for example "Remember, the blocks are for playing with" rather than "Don't throw the blocks".

Praise is extremely important in encouraging positive behaviour. When children feel that they have been rewarded for their behaviour, it encourages them to behave in that way again. This is called positive reinforcement and is linked to Skinner's theory of operant conditioning (see *Theories*).

Rewarding positive behaviour supports children in learning about what is acceptable and appropriate, it makes them feel valued and builds their self-esteem. The most important reward of all is positive attention from caring adults. There are many other ways to reward positive behaviour, including stickers, star charts and badges.

In praising and rewarding children, it is always more effective to be specific rather than generic, for example "I really like how you have used all those colours on your painting", rather than a simple "Well done". This helps children to understand the link between their behaviour and the reward, and they are more likely to do it again.

Case in point

The practitioners at Little Angels Nursery have effective strategies for supporting children's positive behaviour. They use lots of praise and encouragement, including positive language, warm smiles and physical touch to show their approval. They set realistic expectations for behaviour based on their understanding of the children's development and capabilities. Together with the children, the practitioners have developed their 'Golden Rules' about behaviour in the setting, which are positive and based on how the children should behave:

Our 'Golden Rules'

We are gentle and kind

We take care of our toys

We listen to people

We are honest

These 'Golden Rules' are displayed prominently and shared with parents, carers and visitors to the setting.

Summary

Early years practitioners can help children to develop positive behaviour in a variety of ways. They must be good role models and provide children with consistent boundaries. Practitioners also need to understand child development and have realistic expectations of children's behaviour. Having inclusive behaviour policies in the setting, using positive language and giving praise and positive reinforcement will all help children to develop appropriate behaviour patterns.

Reference

STEARNS, J. & WALSH, M. (2011) *Level 2 Certificate for the Children and Young People's Workforce.* London: HarperCollins Publishers.

Positive environments

A positive environment is a place where children feel welcome, safe, valued, interested and challenged. It involves both the people and the space in which children develop and learn, and offers stimulating, inclusive resources, rich learning opportunities and support for children to take risks and explore.

Providing a positive environment

The setting up of a positive environment should consider the indoor and outdoor physical space, the provision of activities and resources, the emotional environment and the regulatory requirements for early years settings.

A positive environment offers access to an outdoor as well as an indoor space and should provide a place where children can explore, learn and develop with the support of sensitive, knowledgeable adults (see *Positive relationships*). It should provide opportunities for children to:

➤ be excited, energetic, adventurous and messy

➤ learn about risk taking

➤ talk, listen, interact and make friends

➤ create, invent, investigate and explore

➤ express ideas and feelings

➤ hide, relax, imagine and reflect.

Providing resources

A positive environment for children includes the provision of resources that will stimulate their interest and meet their individual needs, both indoors and outdoors. For example, by providing a selection of cardboard boxes and fabric, children can choose to create a spaceship, a magic den or a dragon's cave. Resources should be inviting, exciting and safe to use as well as appropriate to the age or stage of development and inclusive, for example resources that represent cultural diversity and are accessible for children with special educational needs (see *Play resources*).

The emotional environment

A positive environment is also very important for children's emotional needs. Children need to feel secure in their surroundings and have a sense of what will happen to them. Having a consistent routine and being cared for by familiar adults helps children feel safe and protected. Practitioners should help children to feel welcome in the setting, greeting them by name with a friendly smile to make them feel at ease.

The setting should be attractive, with inclusive images, displays of children's work and welcoming signs in different languages. Children must feel safe to express their feelings in the setting. Practitioners should support children by sensitively acknowledging emotions and providing appropriate resources for children to express their feelings, such as puppets, natural materials, books and role-play materials (see *Vulnerable children*).

Regulatory requirements

The regulatory requirements for supporting a positive environment in early years settings are outlined in the Statutory Framework for the Early Years Foundation Stage (DfE, 2012). The safeguarding and welfare requirements for early years settings include:

➤ Safety of the premises, toys and equipment

➤ Safety of children, staff and others on the premises in the case of fire or any other emergency

➤ Provision of facilities, including toilets and access for children with special needs

➤ An agreed procedure for security and checking the identity of visitors.

Summary

Children thrive in positive surroundings. They need to feel welcome, safe and stimulated in an environment that supports their learning and development. The space needs to be safe and secure, with well-organised resources and a range of activities. Practitioners need to provide a consistent routine to give children a sense of belonging and help them feel valued in the setting.

References

Department for Education (2012) *Statutory Framework for the Early Years Foundation Stage.* http://www.education.gov.uk

STEARNS, J., SCHMIEDER, C. & MILLAR, E. (2011) *Level 3 Diploma for the Children and Young People's Workforce: Early Learning and Childcare.* London: HarperCollins Publishers.

Positive relationships

Positive relationships is one of the four themes of the Early Years Foundation Stage (DfE, 2012) and it includes relationships between practitioners, children, parents, carers and other professionals. This theme states that positive relationships help children learn to be strong and independent and to feel safe, secure and loved.

Positive relationships with children

Positive relationships with children are warm and loving and foster a sense of belonging. A positive relationship helps a child to feel valued and increases their self-esteem. Within secure relationships, children feel safe to express and understand their feelings and this fosters their emotional and social development. In most early years settings, a child's most important positive relationship will be with their key person, who will take on a special responsibility for their wellbeing in the setting (see *Key person*).

Many different factors help practitioners to develop positive relationships with children, including:

Positive interactions

➤ Providing play experiences and social opportunities for children to talk about their ideas

➤ Responding in a reliable, dependable way and keeping promises

➤ Acknowledging and appreciating children's individual differences

➤ Helping children to express their feelings using books and stories, puppets, painting, dance, music or role-play

➤ Observing children carefully to identify their needs, capabilities and interests.

Listening to children

➤ Paying attention and listening actively to children

➤ Valuing what children have to say and responding sensitively

➤ Using eye contact and positive body language to show genuine interest in what children are saying.

Encouraging choices

➤ Helping children to think for themselves and make their own decisions

➤ Giving children clear information and guidance

➤ Supporting children's decision-making from an early age.

Positive relationships with others

Early years practitioners also need to encourage positive relationships between children. Friendships help children learn how to get on with others, deal with conflicts, share ideas, discuss and argue. Practitioners should provide opportunities for children to collaborate in their play and should involve them in making choices about how children are grouped in the setting.

Early years practitioners also need to be good role models in their relationships with colleagues and others in the setting, including advisors or other professionals, such as health visitors or speech and language therapists (see *Multi-agency working*). It is important for practitioners to form positive relationships with all the people who may be involved in children's care, including parents, grandparents, childminders, foster carers or nannies (see *Parents as partners*).

Barriers to forming positive relationships

It can sometimes be difficult for practitioners to develop positive relationships with children, parents and others. Some of the reasons for this might include:

➤ language and communication difficulties, for example with parents or children who do not speak English

➤ special educational needs, for example children with developmental or behavioural difficulties

➤ religious or cultural differences, for example different values and beliefs

➤ professional differences, for example understanding different professional roles and responsibilities.

Practitioners need to be aware of these potential barriers and develop strategies to overcome them.

Case in point

Yasmin is three years old and today is her first day at nursery. Leena will be her key person and has visited Yasmin at home. She has found out that Yasmin enjoys imaginative play with her soft toys and has suggested that Yasmin should bring her favourite soft toy to nursery with her on her first day. When Yasmin arrives she seems very anxious and is clinging to her mother's coat. Leena crouches down and welcomes Yasmin with a big smile. She acknowledges that Yasmin might feel a bit scared and does not try to rush her. Leena invites Yasmin and her mother into the setting and shows them around. She asks Yasmin what she would like to do and says that her mother can stay as long as she would like to.

Leena is interacting sensitively and respectfully with Yasmin as she starts to develop a positive relationship. She understands that Yasmin needs to build her trust and develop a sense of security and belonging in her new environment.

Summary

Positive relationships are built on trust and respect and enable children to develop confidence and self-esteem. To develop positive relationships with children, practitioners must be sensitive to children's moods and needs. Practitioners should also support the development of positive relationships between children and encourage them to get along with each other. Building positive relationships with parents and other people involved in children's care involves effective communication, active involvement and mutual respect.

References

Department for Education (2012) *Statutory Framework for the Early Years Foundation Stage.* http://www.education.gov.uk

STEARNS, J., SCHMIEDER, C. & MILLAR, E. (2011) *Level 3 Diploma for the Children and Young People's Workforce: Early Learning and Childcare.* London: HarperCollins Publishers.

Prematurity

The World Health Organization defines a premature (or preterm) baby as being born before the 37th week of pregnancy. Premature babies usually have a low birth weight (less than 2.5 kg or 5.5 lb) and frequently need special care which may involve being in a special care baby unit or in an incubator.

Causes of prematurity

According to the UK premature baby charity Bliss, one in every nine babies in the UK is born either prematurely or sick. The majority of preterm births occur without any obvious cause. However, there are some known risks for prematurity including:

➤ Multiple pregnancy

➤ Maternal age (mothers under 20 or over 35 years old have a slightly higher risk of preterm labour)

➤ Impaired foetal development (e.g. growth retardation)

➤ Maternal lifestyle factors (e.g. smoking, a poor diet or engaging in over-strenuous physical activity)

➤ Pre-eclampsia (pregnancy-specific disease associated with high blood pressure)

➤ Previous history of premature birth.

Some babies have a low birth weight even though they are born at full term. This is very common if the mother has smoked during pregnancy. These babies are called 'small for dates' or 'small for gestational age' and they can have some of the same problems associated with prematurity.

Problems associated with prematurity

A premature baby's chance of survival has improved significantly over recent years. However, very premature babies still face a number of health and developmental challenges:

➤ Some premature babies have breathing problems at birth because their lungs did not have enough time to mature before birth.

➤ Premature babies are also four times more likely to die from cot death than babies born with a normal birth weight (see *Cot death*).

➤ Many premature babies face an increased risk of hypothermia (low body temperature). This is because they have a reduced layer of fat under the skin and have difficulty maintaining their body temperature at a constant 37°C.

➤ Premature babies may also experience feeding difficulties and are more vulnerable to infection because their immune system is still immature.

An incubator keeps the baby in a germ-free environment at a constant temperature and provides a means to monitor the baby's breathing. However, having a very tiny baby in an incubator can be a frightening experience for parents and they may need a lot of encouragement to handle and care for their baby in order to feel close and develop an attachment.

Long-term problems

Most premature babies grow up to have no significant health or developmental difficulties. However, some very premature babies may experience long-term problems, including hearing or vision impairment.

Premature babies' development should always be assessed according to their corrected (gestational) age. For example, if the baby was born two months early, they are likely to reach developmental milestones two months later than a full-term baby. Most premature babies will catch up on their developmental milestones within the first year of life.

The EPICure study in 2006 found that some very premature babies experience problems in school, especially with memory, language and problem-solving skills.

The health and development of premature babies is monitored carefully and most premature babies thrive as they grow.

Case in point

Anita went into labour in the 36th week of her pregnancy. Her baby Greg weighed 2 kg at birth and spent five days in the special care baby unit. He was nursed in an incubator where he was constantly observed and his breathing was monitored. Anita and her husband Trevor visited Greg every day, but they were very nervous about touching him because of all the equipment. The staff on the special care unit understand the importance of an attachment relationship in the first few days of life. They encouraged Anita to take Greg out of the incubator and supported her to breast-feed him successfully. They also helped Trevor to change Greg's nappy.

Greg's weight and developmental progress were monitored and he continued to thrive. By the age of six months, both his weight and development were within the range of normal for his chronological age.

Summary

Premature babies need special care because they may have problems with breathing, feeding or maintaining their own body temperature. Most premature babies grow up healthily, but some experience problems and their progress needs to be carefully monitored.

References

BLISS http://www.bliss.org.uk

EPICure (Extremely Premature Infants) Study http://www.epicure.ac.uk

Recording and reporting

Record keeping is a very important aspect of early years practice. Maintaining records helps to ensure that the needs of all children are met and supports the safe and efficient management of the setting. Reporting procedures are equally important in early years settings. Obtaining and sharing information with others enables practitioners to communicate professionally and fulfil their legal obligations.

Recording information

Keeping accurate records is part of the statutory requirement in early years settings and forms an important part of documenting evidence about children. Practitioners have a legal obligation to record certain information about children. Record keeping is also a requirement for registration with government inspectorates, such as Ofsted.

The Statutory Framework for the Early Years Foundation Stage (EYFS) states that records must be easily accessible and that confidential information must be held securely in accordance with the Data Protection Act 1998 (see *Confidentiality*). It also specifies that parents must be given access to all records about their child.

Information may be recorded either electronically or in a paper-based format. Some examples of record keeping which must be undertaken in early years settings include:

➤ Information about the child and family, including who holds parental responsibility, emergency contact details, children's health information (e.g. allergies or medications) and any special educational needs

➤ A daily register of children's attendance

➤ A record of children's progress towards the Early Learning Goals of the EYFS (in England)

➤ A record of administering medicines to children

➤ Details of any accidents or major incidents (e.g. evacuation of the setting).

Reporting procedures

Early years practitioners have a duty to provide information to parents, carers and others involved in children's care, in addition to external organisations and statutory bodies, such as the Health Protection Agency (HPA) (see *Cross-infection*).

The Statutory Framework for the Early Years Foundation Stage (EYFS) states that practitioners should inform parents about the range of activities provided for children, the daily routines of the setting and how parents can share learning at home.

The EYFS also states that settings must have a written procedure for dealing with concerns and complaints from parents. Early years settings have a duty to provide details of their inspection report for parents, and this will also be reported on the inspectorate's website (see *Inspection*).

Most settings also provide regular reports for parents on:

➤ observations and assessments carried out on children

➤ children's developmental progress

➤ daily diaries (particularly for babies).

There are strict procedures for reporting any concerns about children's welfare (see *Safeguarding*) and for informing parents and relevant authorities about the outbreak of any notifiable illnesses (for example, meningitis) or accidents occurring in the setting.

In England, early years settings are required to provide reports about children's progress within the EYFS. This includes a written report summarising children's development at the age of two years in addition to the Early Years Foundation Stage Profile (EYFSP) at the end of the foundation stage. A copy of the EYFSP should be given to the parents, the local authority and the school the child will attend (see *EYFS*). Information may be reported verbally, electronically or written in a paper-based format.

Case in point

It is particularly important to record and report any incident involving a head injury to a child. Even though it may not seem serious at the time, any injury to the head can potentially be life-threatening. Most early years settings will use some form of written head injury notification to provide information for parents about possible serious symptoms, as shown here:

Notification of Head Injury

Date: _____   Name of child: _____

Description of accident and/or injury: _____
_____
_____

If your child experiences any of the following symptoms, you should consult your doctor without delay:

Headache
Nausea or vomiting
Dizziness
Blurred vision

Signed:

Summary

Recording and reporting procedures provide a system for documenting evidence in early years settings. Record keeping is part of the statutory requirement, and reporting procedures help practitioners maintain communication with parents, carers and others involved in children's care.

References

Data Protection Act 1998 (c. 29). London: The Stationery Office. http://www.legislation.gov.uk

Department for Education (2012) *Statutory Framework for the Early Years Foundation Stage*. http://www.education.gov.uk

Ofsted http://www.ofsted.gov.uk

Reflective practice

Reflective practice describes the process of observing, questioning and revising working systems and procedures. The key aims of reflective practice in early years are to enhance professional growth, enrich the quality of provision and improve outcomes for children and their families. The process involves practitioners in monitoring their working practices, evaluating and reviewing the evidence and making improvements.

The importance of reflective practice

Reflective practice enables practitioners to identify working patterns and view them from a different perspective. It also supports practitioners to challenge assumptions, ask questions, test ideas and plan to implement changes. It is important because it enables practitioners to:

➤ plan effective early learning experiences based on children's individual needs

➤ be analytical and proactive in making informed decisions about practice in the setting

➤ engage in constructive dialogue with colleagues and other professionals

➤ develop a holistic understanding of early years practice.

Reflective practice also forms the basis of continuous quality improvement for the provision of early years care and education, and can help practitioners to change aspects of their practice, including the way they think and how they do things.

Developing reflective practice

Practitioners can improve their practice in many different ways using a variety of sources, for example observing or work shadowing a senior colleague, engaging in professional discussions and reading articles or research reports in journals or online. Practitioners may also attend conferences, workshops and seminars or visit centres of excellence to observe best practice. The process of regular supervision to meet and discuss performance with a manager or senior colleague can be very useful in highlighting professional development needs and helping to identify sources of training or further education.

Professional development

Many practitioners create a learning journal or professional development record, which can be a useful tool for reflective thinking. This helps them to objectively measure their own performance against best practice and to identify aspects of their practice that require further development, for example:

Reflection on practice	Evidence	How can I improve my practice?	Where can I find information to help me?
How well do I record observations of children's learning and development?			
How well do I interact with babies to stimulate their communication?			

With this kind of information, practitioners can plan and make the necessary changes to improve their practice. Action planning helps practitioners to focus their ideas and decide what steps are needed to achieve their goals.

Effective action planning involves SMART objective setting:

- **S**pecific (Precise; detailed; directed; describing exactly what is to be done)

- **M**easurable (Observable; quantifiable; assessing exactly what has been done)

- **A**chievable (Can it be done? Do you have the skills?)

- **R**ealistic (Is it possible, considering the resources available?)

- **T**ime limited (With specific times for review, evaluation and completion).

Case in point

An example of a SMART objective would be:

'To use the "Development Matters" statements in the EYFS to assess the physical development of three children, before 10 September.'

This is a SMART objective because it:

➤ identifies the assessment tool being used (specific)

➤ identifies how many children are to be assessed and uses a standard scale (measurable)

➤ is something that is both possible to do (achievable) and likely to happen (realistic)

➤ identifies the timescale in which the assessments will happen (time limited).

The objective would not be SMART if it simply said: 'To assess the children's physical development'.

Summary

Anyone who works with children should think about how effectively they are doing their job and if there are any ways they could improve. Reflective practice is an ongoing process, which provides opportunities for practitioners to learn from experience, analyse their practice and make improvements in their provision. Repeating this process creates a continuous cycle of improvement which impacts on the learning, development and care experiences provided for children in the setting.

References

PAIGE-SMITH, A. & CRAFT, A. (2011) *Developing Reflective Practice in the Early Years*. 2nd Ed. Maidenhead: Open University Press.

STEARNS, J., SCHMIEDER, C. & YOUNG, K. (2013) *BTEC National Children's Play, Learning and Development*. London: HarperCollins Publishers.

Regression

In early years, the term regression is used to describe going backwards to an earlier stage of development. Children often regress when they feel emotionally vulnerable or threatened.

Emotional development

The process of emotional development is complex. It takes time for children to develop security and self-confidence, and most children will usually experience some obstacles along the way. When faced with unfamiliar situations, it is natural for children to express their anxiety and insecurity, for example when starting school or nursery for the first time or dealing with a new baby in the family.

When a child 'regresses', they go backwards to an earlier stage of emotional development. They might, for example, start to wet themselves again rather than using the toilet, or go back to 'baby talk' and sucking their thumb.

A child who feels insecure may also develop low self-esteem and feel unloved. As a result, the child may struggle to express or control their emotions and their insecurities might be expressed through aggressive or attention-seeking behaviour (see *Challenging behaviour*).

Supporting children

Regression is a normal stage in child development and it is important to support children through this difficult phase. Children who are feeling emotionally insecure need to know that they are valued and loved, and should be given lots of positive encouragement and reassurance. In order to feel secure, children need consistent boundaries, familiarity and routine. This helps to boost children's confidence and build their self-esteem.

Children should not be punished for regressive behaviour, but should be supported with patience. Regression is usually temporary and the more tolerance children are shown, the better they will handle insecure situations (see *Positive behaviour*).

Case in point

Myles is three and a half years old and has always been a cheerful, confident and very lovable boy. This has all changed, however, since baby Amy was born last month. Myles has become clingy and whining, and refuses to cooperate with daily routines, such as getting washed and dressed. He has started to wet the bed at night (something he hasn't done for almost a year now) and he wants his mother all the time. He always used to enjoy going to playgroup, but now he doesn't want to leave the house and he has even started to suck his thumb.

Myles is showing some classic signs of regressive behaviour. He should be supported with lots of positive attention, praise and encouragement. Myles's mother should spend some time alone with him every day, to reinforce that she loves him just as much as she ever did. She could also encourage him to care for the baby and 'help' her. Myles should not be punished for wetting the bed or sucking his thumb. These behaviours will soon pass if Myles is treated with love and consistency.

Summary

Supporting children who are experiencing regression can be very challenging. Young children express their feelings through their behaviour and when they feel insecure, this can sometimes be misunderstood and is often interpreted as being 'naughty'. Early years practitioners need to understand that regressive behaviour is usually temporary and children need to be treated with love and consistency.

Research in early years

Research in early years helps to support the provision of services and improve outcomes for children and their families. Practitioners can use the findings from research in early years to implement new ideas and improve their practice. Conducting their own research enables practitioners to investigate new approaches and assess the effectiveness of their work.

Types of research

Many different types of research are used in early years, employing a variety of research methods. Some of the different types of research include:

➤ Action research: improving professional practice with a practical focus

➤ Longitudinal research: monitoring progress or change over a long period of time

➤ Primary research: collecting data using primary research methods (e.g. questionnaires)

➤ Secondary research: studying material that has already been written and conducting a literature review.

Qualitative research focuses on thoughts and opinions rather than facts, whereas quantitative research focuses on numbers and statistics that can be measured and analysed.

Ethical issues in research

Any kind of research involving children and families will be subject to ethical considerations. Young children are vulnerable and much of the information involved in the research will be sensitive and private. Research in early years should therefore be mindful of issues such as confidentiality, data protection and children's rights (see *Rights of children*).

Research methodology

Most research in early years involves a combination of primary and secondary research methods. As a secondary research method, a literature review will provide background material and information about the subject. It should include a variety of different sources, including books, government reports, research articles and internet-based information. Primary research methods used in early years include:

➤ Questionnaires: these can be used to obtain facts and opinions and can be a valuable method of collecting a wide range of information from many individuals.

➤ Interviews: these are often used to collect qualitative data. Some interviews can be conducted by telephone or email, but are most effective in person.

➤ Case studies: these are detailed investigations into the background of individual children or families and can be useful for examining specific issues, for example researching the experience of having a child with Attention Deficit Hyperactivity Disorder (ADHD).

➤ Naturalistic observation: this is widely used as a research method, particularly for studying children's behaviour. A camera or digital recording device would generally be used to record the observations, which can then be analysed using a rating scale or checklist.

The research process

The research process requires skilful planning and efficient time management. It involves collating and summarising data, analysing findings and writing a research report, which evaluates the process and makes recommendations for implementation. Findings from research in early years might indicate a need for:

➤ better ways of working
➤ new methods of carrying out routine tasks

➤ more staff training in a particular area

➤ changes to local early years services or national policies.

Case in point

Cindy is a senior practitioner in an early years setting. She wants to investigate the quality of attachment relationships between babies under one year and their key person. Cindy sets up a small-scale research project and uses naturalistic observations to study the interactions. She uses a checklist to record the frequency of their regular interactions, including smiling, eye contact and playful communication.

As a result of her research, Cindy recommends the following changes to practice in her early years setting:

➤ Specific time should be set aside every day for each key person to give undivided attention to the babies in their care.

➤ Music, rhyme and singing together should feature prominently every day.

➤ All aspects of personal care (e.g. feeding, nappy changing) should be carried out by the key person wherever possible.

➤ There should be more staff training provided on the role of the key person, the importance of attachment and interactive play with babies.

Summary

Research plays an extremely important role in early years practice. It continually extends knowledge and aids professional reflection. The implementation of research can lead to improvements in professional practice and inform policy making at both local and national levels.

Reference

STEARNS, J., SCHMIEDER, C. & YOUNG, K. (2013) *BTEC National Children's Play, Learning and Development*. London: HarperCollins Publishers.

Resilience

Resilience is the ability to deal with the ups and downs of life and the capacity to recover from setbacks. It comes from secure early attachments and positive relationships and is a key component of the prime area of Personal, Social and Emotional Development within the Early Years Foundation Stage (DfE, 2012).

Developing resilience

It is widely recognised that resilient children are more confident, have a positive sense of wellbeing and are less vulnerable to abuse or harm. Early years practitioners can support the development of resilience in children in many different ways, including:

➤ Encouraging children's efforts as well as praising their achievements

➤ Including children in decision-making and providing realistic choices so they can feel in control

➤ Listening with respect and interest and responding with warmth and patience

➤ Setting realistic challenges so children can do things they feel proud of and achieve

➤ Providing routines and consistent boundaries so children feel secure and know what is expected of them.

Resilience and emotional wellbeing

Resilience forms a key element of children's emotional wellbeing and self-esteem. Daniel Goleman incorporated this into his ideas on 'emotional intelligence' and highlighted the main principles as the development of:

➤ self-awareness

➤ the ability to manage feelings

➤ motivation and enthusiasm to learn

➤ empathy

➤ social skills and the ability to relate to others.

Research has shown that resilient children are better able to cope with difficult and distressing situations, for example bereavement or parental divorce, as well as events such as starting school or having a new baby in the family (see *Transitions*).

Case in point

Ryan is four years old and an only child. His parents recently divorced as a result of his father's drug misuse, and his father is now in prison. Ryan is currently living with his mother and maternal grandmother.

Ryan had always been an outgoing, boisterous boy, who enjoyed football and social play with his friends. However, he has recently become increasingly withdrawn and uncooperative, he refuses to participate in games and is negative in his approach.

Ryan is coping with a lot of changes in his life. To help Ryan develop resilience, he needs positive attention, consistent routines and boundaries to help him feel secure. Ryan should also be involved in making decisions so he feels more in control of his life. He needs praise and encouragement to build his self-esteem and to feel valued and listened to. Most of all, Ryan needs opportunities to express his confusion, anger and sadness through play experiences, such as painting, role-play and puppets.

In this way, Ryan can be supported to become more resilient and deal with everything that is happening in his life.

Summary

Children's emotional health is just as important as their physical health and helping children to develop resilience can positively influence their life chances. Early years practitioners have a responsibility to provide emotional support in order to promote positive outcomes for children.

References

Action for Children http://www.actionforchildren.org.uk

Department for Education (2012) *Statutory Framework for the Early Years Foundation Stage.* http://www.education.gov.uk

GOLEMAN, D. (1996) *Emotional Intelligence: Why It Can Matter More Than IQ.* London: Bantam Doubleday Dell Publishing Group.

STEARNS, J., SCHMIEDER, C. & YOUNG, K. (2013) *BTEC National Children's Play, Learning and Development.* London: HarperCollins Publishers.

Rights of children

Rights are entitlements that are protected by law. The rights of children are set out in the United Nations Convention on the Rights of the Child (UNCRC) (UNICEF, 1989). This convention sets out 54 articles, covering issues such as children's rights to privacy, health care and access to information. Early years practitioners should help children understand their rights and always act in the best interests of the children in their care.

UNCRC

All children have the same rights. The United Nations Convention applies to all children, whatever their race, religion or abilities and whatever type of family they come from. Some of the articles outlining the rights of children include:

➤ Discrimination: no child should be treated unfairly for any reason

➤ Respect: children have the right to be consulted about decisions affecting them

➤ Protection: children have the right to be protected from being hurt and mistreated, physically or mentally

➤ Disability: children who have any kind of disability have the right to special care and support

➤ Health care: children have the right to good quality health care, safe drinking water, nutritious food and a clean and safe environment

➤ Play: children have the right to relax and play.

Duty of care

A duty of care is a legal term, which refers to the responsibilities of adults to support the wellbeing of others. This is implicit in the UNCRC and is particularly important in relation to young children who are too young to protect themselves. The specific responsibilities for early years practitioners include:

➤ Upholding children's rights and protecting them from discrimination

➤ Meeting children's needs and promoting their interests

➤ Protecting children's health, safety and wellbeing

➤ Ensuring safe practice and being aware of legislation.

A duty of care will be included in many of the policies and procedures in early years settings (see *Policies and procedures*).

Case in point

At Little Rascals Nursery, the staff team understand the importance of the rights of children. The setting has clear policies about equality, discrimination and inclusive practice, and thorough policies relating to the children's health, safety and wellbeing. The children are included in creating the rules about behaviour in the setting and practitioners encourage all the children to respect each other. Planning is based on observations of the children's individual needs and interests and the children are fully involved in making their own decisions about food choices, activities and play experiences.

Mari, who uses a wheelchair, is fully supported by an Individual Education Plan and the Special Educational Needs Coordinator. This enables Mari to access facilities and participate in play activities both inside and outside of the setting.

The practitioners at Little Rascals make strong links with parents and the local community. This helps to create meaningful connections with families from a wide range of different backgrounds and supports the setting in meeting children's individual needs.

Summary

Young children are particularly vulnerable and have specific rights that recognise their special need for protection. By recognising children's rights in this way, the United Nations Convention firmly sets the focus on the whole child and offers a vision for all children to develop their full potential.

Reference

UNICEF (UK) (1989) *United Nations Convention on the Rights of the Child.* http://www.unicef.org.uk

Risk assessment

The process of risk assessment aims to identify potential risks (dangers) to the health, safety and security of children, practitioners and visitors who use early years settings, and to implement measures to minimise the possible risks. Early years practitioners are required by law to carry out formal risk assessments for both the indoor and outdoor environment and for any visits outside of the setting.

The risk assessment process

Within the setting

Early years practitioners should make daily routine inspections to assess both the indoor and outdoor environment in the setting, for example checking that fire escapes are clear, all toys and equipment are in good working order and outdoor play areas are safe and secure.

A formal risk assessment uses a structure to identify and assess the risk, and helps find ways to avoid or reduce the risk to an acceptable level. It will generally involve the following steps:

1. Identify hazards.

2. Identify who is at risk.

3. Evaluate the risk and take measures to reduce it.

4. Record findings and implement an action plan.

5. Review and monitor on a regular basis.

The risk assessment process should be accurately recorded and should identify the potential hazards, possible risks and an action plan (see *Recording and reporting*).

Visits away from the setting

There are different risks involved when taking children on visits away from the setting. For example, the outing may involve travelling on public transport or the children being

engaged in different activities, such as having a picnic.
Practitioners must follow the policies and procedures
for safety on outings and a full risk assessment must be
completed including:

➤ An assessment of required adult-to-child ratios for
supervision

➤ The hazards that may be encountered and precautions
that should be taken

➤ An assessment of the weather conditions and how
these will be accommodated

➤ Any specific, individual needs of the children (e.g.
allergies or other medical conditions)

➤ The times of departure and return to the setting and
communication arrangements

➤ A register of all the children attending

➤ Procedures to follow in an emergency (see *Policies and
procedures*).

Balancing the risk

Many things in life carry
some element of risk.
Young children need
to learn how to take
risks safely. This requires
a realistic approach
and a certain amount
of common sense. If
children are constantly
protected from risk,
they are denied the
opportunity to practise
risk taking.

Early years practitioners are responsible for keeping children safe while also providing them with challenging environments in which to play and learn. This involves an assessment of the environment and the nature of the activity, in addition to an understanding of children's development and capabilities.

Experienced early years practitioners become skilled at assessing and managing risk so that they can provide challenging activities for children to explore and take risks in a safe, supported environment. In many settings, adults will complete risk assessments with children to model the process to them.

Case in point

The children at Treetops Nursery are going to plant bulbs outside in the nursery garden. The deputy manager has conducted a risk assessment for this activity and has identified the following hazards:

1. Children will be using gardening tools and digging in the soil.

2. Children will be exposed to the weather, insects and potentially dangerous objects, such as broken glass or dog faeces.

3. Children's security is more vulnerable outdoors.

Having identified these hazards, she has itemised the following risks for the children, staff and parent helpers:

1. injury

2. infection

3. sunburn

4. bee/wasp stings or insect bites

5. children wandering off the premises.

The deputy manager has outlined an action plan on the risk assessment as follows:

1. Check the garden and outdoor area for any hazards and remove if necessary; check security of fencing and locks on gates and make secure.

2. Encourage the children to practise using gardening tools beforehand (e.g. in their play).

3. Check staff and children's health records for any bee or wasp allergies, and take necessary precautions.

4. Check the weather; apply sunscreen and supply sunhats or rainwear if necessary.

5. Ensure sufficient staff members are present to supervise the children at all times.

Summary

Risk assessment is an ongoing process in early years settings. It should include checks on the premises, equipment and planned activities as well as outings away from the setting. The risk assessment process enables practitioners to recognise potential risks before harm occurs and take measures to avoid or minimise the impact. Early years practitioners need to balance the assessment of risk with the need to provide children with challenge in order to support play, learning and development.

Reference

Health and Safety Executive http://www.hse.gov.uk

Safeguarding

The term 'safeguarding' refers to the practices employed by practitioners to ensure children are kept safe and free from all kinds of harm. Safeguarding children's welfare involves protecting them from abuse, promoting their interests, keeping them safe and protecting their rights. Early years practitioners have a legal responsibility to safeguard children's welfare by providing high quality early years settings that are welcoming, safe and stimulating, where children are able to enjoy learning and grow in confidence.

Promoting children's welfare

The safeguarding and welfare requirements in England apply to all types of early years settings and can be found in the Statutory Framework for the Early Years Foundation Stage (see *EYFS*). This mandatory guidance clearly states that providers must take all necessary steps to:

➤ safeguard children's welfare

➤ ensure the suitability of adults who have contact with children

➤ maintain the safety and suitability of premises, environment and equipment

➤ promote good health and manage children's behaviour

➤ maintain records, policies and procedures.

Protecting children

All children have a right to grow up in safety and adults have a duty to protect them from being harmed or abused in any way (see *Rights of children*).

Early years practitioners must ensure the supervision and safety of children, both indoors and on visits outside of the setting. This includes maintaining a safe, secure environment, conducting risk assessments and having policies and procedures in place to prevent accidents and control the spread of infection (see *Risk assessment*).

Child abuse can take many different forms, including neglect and physical, emotional and sexual abuse, all of which can have a devastating effect on children's health, development, wellbeing and future lives. Practitioners must be vigilant for signs of abuse, which might include physical signs, such as bruising, constant tiredness or changes in the child's appearance or behaviour.

Legislation, policies and procedures

The legal responsibilities of early years practitioners are outlined in the government document *Working Together to Safeguard Children* (DfE, 2013). Early years settings must have clear policies and procedures to safeguard children and protect staff. This includes issues like:

➤ staff recruitment

➤ safe working practices and security measures

➤ responding to concerns about abuse

➤ reporting and sharing information and data protection (see *Recording and reporting*).

Responding to concerns

Any concerns about the welfare of a child will always be fully investigated. This may come as a result of disclosure about an abusive situation by the child or from the suspicions of a member of staff. The investigation will usually involve a meeting of all the professionals involved with the family in a Child Protection Conference, held on behalf of the Local Safeguarding Children Board. The purpose of this conference is to create the Child Protection Plan, which will outline the multi-agency support required to safeguard and promote the welfare of the child (see *Multi-agency working*).

Case in point

The safeguarding policy at Tufton Park children's centre clearly outlines the arrangements for confirming the identity of parents or carers who are collecting children and checking the identity of any visitors to the setting.

Jo works at Tufton Park and is responsible for a small group of 'key children' whom she knows very well. At the end of one day, Jo is busy putting some playthings away and notices an unfamiliar man has come to collect David, aged four. The man says that he is David's uncle and he has been asked by David's mother to pick him up. Jo asks the man to wait in the parents' room and she goes to check with the manager of the setting. The manager contacts David's mother for confirmation and clarifies the identity of the man before allowing David to leave with him.

Summary

Young children are extremely vulnerable and rely on adults to promote their welfare. This includes providing food and nurture as well as ensuring their security and keeping them safe from neglect or harm. Early years practitioners must be aware of safeguarding procedures and know how to respond to any concerns about children's welfare or safety.

References

Department for Education (2011) *The Munro Review of Child Protection: Final Report*. http://www.education.gov.uk

Department for Education (2012) *Statutory Framework for the Early Years Foundation Stage*. http://www.education.gov.uk

Department for Education (2013) *Working Together to Safeguard Children: A Guide to Inter-agency Working to Safeguard and Promote the Welfare of Children*. http://www.education.gov.uk

National Society for the Prevention of Cruelty to Children (NSPCC) http://www.nspcc.org.uk

Schemas

'Schemas are patterns of linked behaviours, which the child can generalise and use in a whole variety of situations. It is best to think of schemas as being a cluster of pieces which fit together.' (Bruce, 2011)

A schema is often described as a mental structure or a pattern of behaviour, which children explore at different levels and in a variety of situations to support their cognitive development.

Identifying schemas

Schemas develop in clusters. Sometimes they are very obvious, sometimes they seem to disappear. Children who appear to be flitting from one activity to another may, in fact, be exploring an idea in depth, for example how they can move things from one place to another.

Children exhibit their schemas dynamically through movements, such as dancing or climbing, and constructively in their drawings, paintings and models. Schemas should be observed and used in planning activities to extend children's learning and development. Examples of schemas include:

➤ Transporting: a child may carry all the bricks from one place to another in a bag, or move toys around in pushchairs or wheelbarrows

➤ Enveloping: a child may cover themselves with a cloth when washing, wrap a doll in a blanket or cover their whole painting with one colour

➤ Rotation: a child may be fascinated by the spinning washing machine, anything with wheels, rolling down a hill or spinning around and around

➤ Trajectory: a child may be fascinated by the flow of water from a pipe, throwing objects or a ball and watching its flight through the air, or dropping things from a height and watching them fall

> Positioning: a child may put things on their head, lie on the floor or under the table, or line up toys in rows or on top of one another.

Schemas in learning and development

Chris Athey was a constructivist who developed Piaget's ideas about schemas in relation to children's learning (see *Theories*). Athey identified four stages that children go through in exploring and using schemas:

> A period of physical action where the movement does not carry any real significance; for example, a child spinning round and round without any specific purpose

> Using schemas to symbolise something; for example, the spinning is used to symbolise being on a roundabout

> Beginning to see the functional relationship between two things; for example, connecting the spinning of the washing machine with drying the clothes

> Using schemas to support thought; for example, the child puts all of these ideas into words and expresses the reasoning behind spinning.

Case in point

Chloe's key person makes the following observation of Chloe:

Chloe is three and a half years old. She is playing in the role-play area, dressing up in a cloak and a big scarf. Chloe then wraps the baby doll in a blanket and places it in the pushchair. She pushes the doll around the setting and back into the role-play area, where she puts the doll into the cot, wrapping more blankets around it. Then she puts the doll back into the pushchair, pushes it outside into the garden, and takes it out again and buries it in a pile of leaves.

Playing outdoors, later in the week:

Chloe holds the hosepipe with two hands, directing water into a bucket, which contains some sand. Chloe puts her finger in the flow of water at the end of the hosepipe, which increases the water pressure. She moves the hosepipe nearer, making the water swirl in the bucket and the sand swirl around in the water. Chloe watches, then repeats her actions with the next bucket in line. She carries the buckets inside, one at a time, lining them up in the construction play area.

Careful observation of Chloe might identify enveloping, trajectory and transporting schemas in her play, which could be monitored over time and used in planning further activities to extend Chloe's learning and development.

Summary

Observing schemas in children's play and behaviour can help early years practitioners to identify stages in children's learning. This can help in planning appropriate experiences and activities to meet children's individual interests and extend their play, learning and development.

References

BRUCE, T. (2011) *Early Childhood Education*. London: Hodder Education.

STEARNS, J., SCHMIEDER, C. & YOUNG, K. (2013) *BTEC National Children's Play, Learning and Development*. London: HarperCollins Publishers.

SEN

Children are defined as having special educational needs (SEN) if they need more help than most children of the same age to make progress or to access learning. These children need extra help because of a range of needs, such as physical disabilities, learning difficulties, sensory impairment, emotional and behavioural difficulties or problems with speech and language.

Definition of SEN

The term 'special educational needs' has a legal definition, which states that children may have difficulties with:

➤ reading, writing, number work or understanding information

➤ expressing themselves or understanding what others are saying

➤ making friends or relating to adults

➤ behaving appropriately in school

➤ sensory or physical needs which may affect them in school.

The law states that children do not have learning difficulties because their first language is not English or because they have a health problem or medical condition, such as diabetes. These children are usually referred to as having 'additional needs' (DfE, 2001).

Models of disability

There are two different views of disability that have influenced current early years practice:

1. The medical model views a child's disability as a medical problem that can be treated. This model is considered

to be quite outdated, as it emphasises what the child cannot do rather than focusing on the child's individual needs.

2. The social model views disability in the context of the people and the environment in which a child lives. It focuses on children's strengths and ways to meet their individual needs.

Supporting children with SEN

There are different stages of support for children with SEN in early years settings, including:

➤ Early Years Action, discussion with the Special Educational Needs Coordinator (SENCo) and writing an Individual Education Plan (IEP)

➤ Early Years Action Plus, with additional help from an external specialist, e.g. a speech and language therapist, or with a support worker in the setting

➤ Assessment of the child's needs by professionals from different agencies

➤ A statement of special educational needs outlining the child's needs and how they should be met.

The Statutory Framework for the Early Years Foundation Stage (EYFS) in England states that settings must promote equality of opportunity for children in their care, including support for children with SEN or disabilities. This means adapting or differentiating activities to enable all children to take part, providing suitable, specialist resources, such as mobility aids or interactive technology, and completing (with the parents) an IEP for the child (see *Inclusive practice*).

The SENCo

In most early years settings, the Special Educational Needs Coordinator (SENCo) is an experienced practitioner who has an interest in children with SEN. The role of the SENCo includes:

➤ Communicating with the child's key person and the parents

➤ Helping to write the child's IEP and advising staff on its implementation

➤ Organising support from external agencies

➤ Facilitating specialist resources and activities.

One of the main roles of the SENCo is to signpost children and families to other specialists who can provide help and support, for example a speech and language therapist, behavioural support worker or physiotherapist.

Case in point

Jamilla is three years old and has cerebral palsy. She uses a wheelchair and cannot walk unaided, but she has good use of her arms and hands. Jamilla loves music and enjoys singing familiar songs and rhymes.

The SENCo in the early years setting has created an IEP with Jamilla's parents, which outlines Jamilla's individual needs and how they can best be met. The SENCo has also provided a special table, which Jamilla can use with her wheelchair, along with a special support for her back and neck.

Jamilla's key person, Christina, provides lots of tactile experiences, including play dough, which helps to develop the strength in Jamilla's fingers. Christina plays music for Jamilla and helps her to 'dance' in her wheelchair. Christina takes Jamilla outside in her wheelchair and encourages the other children to include Jamilla in throwing and catching balls and some of their other games.

Summary

Early years practitioners have a responsibility to meet the needs of all the children in their care. Children with SEN have very particular needs and practitioners should work closely with specialists and the child's parents to support the child's learning and enable them to reach their full potential.

References

Department for Education (2001) *Special Educational Needs Code of Practice.* http://www.education.gov.uk

Department for Education (2011) *Support and Aspiration: A New Approach to Special Educational Needs and Disability.* Cm 8027. http://www.education.gov.uk

Department for Education (2012) *Statutory Framework for the Early Years Foundation Stage.* http://www.education.gov.uk

Stages of play

In 1932, Mildred Parten observed children between the ages of two and five engaged in free play. She categorised six stages of play, which highlighted how children's developing social skills are reflected in their play.

The six stages of play

The six stages of play as defined by Mildred Parten help early years practitioners to plan meaningful activities for children, which help to promote their social development through play.

1. Unoccupied play: the child is not actually playing, but just observing the play of others. This is more common in infants and very young children.

2. Solitary (independent play): the child appears unaware or uninterested in the play of others and totally absorbed in their own activity. This is more common in younger children (aged two to three years).

3. Onlooker play: the child shows interest in the play of others by looking on or commenting, but does not join in. This is more common in younger children.

4. Parallel (adjacent play): the child plays separately from others but close to them, and will mimic their play behaviour. This is often seen as a transitory stage to more social and cooperative play.

5. Associative play: the child is more interested in the social interactions of other children

than the play activity itself. The play may appear random and unorganised or there may be no play activity at all.

6. Cooperative play: the child is interested both in the other children playing and in the play activity itself, which is often highly organised with children performing assigned roles. This is relatively uncommon in pre-school children as it requires the most social maturity and high levels of social skills, such as cooperating and negotiating. However, many more mature four-year-olds will display this type of play.

Through play, children learn and practise many basic social skills. They develop a sense of self and learn how to interact with other children and how to make friends. Children also learn about sharing, cooperating and building relationships.

Early years practitioners need to observe the stages of children's play carefully. This helps them to plan appropriate and meaningful activities to develop children's development and learning.

Summary

Through play, children learn and practise many basic social skills. They develop a sense of self, learn to interact with other children and discover how to make friends. Parten's theory about the stages of play continues to reinforce our understanding of the connection between children's play and their social development.

Reference

STEARNS, J., SCHMIEDER, C. & YOUNG, K. (2013) *BTEC National Children's Play, Learning and Development.* London: HarperCollins Publishers.

Theories

Current early years practice is based on years of theoretical knowledge, which helps practitioners to understand children's learning, development and behaviour. These theories form the foundation on which many of the early years frameworks are based. It is important for early years practitioners to understand theoretical models and to use these ideas to inform their professional practice.

Theories about children's learning and behaviour

Many different theoretical models inform our understanding of children's learning and behaviour. In general, these can be divided into three different approaches: behaviourism, constructivism and social learning theory.

Behaviourism

This model is based on the idea that learning happens as a result of responses to events which cause changes in behaviour. The theorists Ivan Pavlov and Burrhus Frederic Skinner were both behaviourists and they described different forms of conditioning. Pavlov described classical conditioning as a form of learning where behaviour changes as a result of a response to a stimulus, for example when children learn to respond immediately when they hear the fire alarm in school.

Skinner's approach (operant conditioning) is particularly relevant to our ideas about shaping children's behaviour as it rests on the principle that positive reinforcement helps children to develop socially acceptable behaviour; if behaviour is rewarded, then it is likely to be repeated.

Behaviourism underpins current early years practice through the use of praise and encouragement, stickers and other rewards in order to encourage appropriate behaviour in children (see *Positive behaviour*).

Constructivism

This model is based on the idea that learning happens as a result of practical, hands-on activity and that children build (or construct) their own knowledge through their experiences. It is built on the principle of starting from where the child is at to facilitate learning. The theorists Jean Piaget, Lev Vygotsky and Jerome Bruner were constructivists. However, Vygotsky and Bruner differed from Piaget considerably in their thinking.

Constructivism underpins current early years practice by emphasising the importance of active learning through play (see *Active learning*). The role of the adult is to scaffold children's learning through sensitive interactions and open-ended questions, and to encourage creative, critical thinking (see *Creative, critical thinking*).

Piaget is often referred to as the 'Father of Constructivism'. He stated that children's cognitive development progresses in four distinct stages:

1. Sensori-motor (birth–2 years)

2. Pre-operational (2–7 years)

3. Concrete operational (7–11 years)

4. Formal operational (11–15 years).

Piaget believed that children learn principally from working things out for themselves. He developed ideas about children's schemas (see *Schemas*), egocentricity (see *Egocentric*) and their ability to understand concepts (see *Concepts*). Although Piaget's work is considered as fundamental to our understanding of child development, it has also been questioned in the recent past. Now it is not considered to explain sufficiently how children learn.

Vygotsky and Bruner believed that children need interaction from adults or more mature peers to maximise their learning, and that social interaction is crucial to good learning. They were called social constructivists.

Social learning theory

This model is based on the idea that learning happens as a result of observing and imitating others. It emphasises the importance of the learning environment and of adults being good role models for children. Albert Bandura developed this approach and his ideas have influenced more modern theorists, such as Tina Bruce.

Theories about children's language development

There are many different theories about children's language development, which have direct relevance for early years practitioners.

Noam Chomsky supports a nativist view (see *Nature and nurture*). He claims that children do not simply learn language through imitation alone, but are born with an innate ability to learn languages, which he calls the 'Language Acquisition Device' (LAD). In contrast, Roger Brown focused on the development of children's language through different stages, based on their understanding of language use.

Theories about children's emotional development

John Bowlby's attachment theory is one of the most significant theories about children's emotional development. He emphasised the importance of young children developing a strong attachment relationship (emotional connection) with their main carer and the significance of this attachment for children's security, self-esteem and emotional development (see *Attachment*).

Bowlby's attachment theory forms the basis of the key person approach in early years settings (see *Key person*) and helps practitioners to support children who are dealing with transitions (see *Transitions*).

Ecological systems theory

This approach was developed by Urie Bronfenbrenner and emphasises the influence of environmental factors, such as the family, local community and wider society, on children's development.

Ecological systems theory highlights the importance of working in partnership with parents, supporting children's learning in the home and planning activities based on what children do with their family and in their community (see *Parents as partners*).

Summary

Theory underpins and guides every aspect of work in early years. Experienced practitioners use a combination of different theoretical approaches to inform their professional practice to support children's play, learning and development.

Reference

STEARNS, J., SCHMIEDER, C. & YOUNG, K. (2013) *BTEC National Children's Play, Learning and Development*. London: HarperCollins Publishers.

Toilet training

Toilet training refers to the process whereby children develop the ability to use the toilet independently. Control of the bladder and bowels relies on the maturing nervous system and the child gaining control of their muscles. All children do this at different times.

Transition from nappies

Most children will start to indicate their toilet needs between 18 months and two years old and can be taught to use the toilet rather than relying on a nappy. Some of the signs that a child is ready might include:

➤ Long periods when the nappy is dry

➤ Pulling at their nappy to indicate it is wet or dirty

➤ Understanding and using words to say they need the toilet

➤ Interest in other children using the toilet.

Children usually learn to control their bowels before their bladder and girls tend to be ready for toilet training sooner than boys of the same age. A child must be ready and interested, and it is important to give praise and encouragement throughout the whole process. Establishing a regular toileting routine, such as after mealtimes, can also help children with this transition.

Developing independence

Supporting children to become independent in using the toilet can be frustrating. A positive attitude towards toilet training will help the child gain confidence and independence. Most children have setbacks before they are fully confident and it is important not to punish children for these accidents.

Some children prefer to use a potty, but others may choose to start using the toilet straightaway. A child's toilet seat and a step stool can help children to be more independent.

Children should be encouraged to wash their hands each time they use the potty or toilet to reinforce good hygiene practice (see *Cross-infection*). By three years old, most children are dry during the day although it can take longer to gain control throughout the night. As children gain independence and start using the toilet on their own, they may still need help with their clothing or wiping their bottoms. However, most children will be fully independent with their toileting by the age of five years.

Case in point

Mari is 20 months old and attends Treetops Nursery. Hannah, Mari's key person, has noticed recently that Mari gets upset when her nappy is wet. She pulls at it and comes over to Hannah for attention. Hannah has spoken to Mari's mother about this and they have decided that it may be a good time to start toilet training.

Hannah has put Mari's potty in a special place in the children's toileting area. Every time Mari indicates that her nappy needs changing, Hannah sits her on the potty and gives her lots of praise and encouragement. Hannah encourages Mari to use her potty after every meal and to wash her hands each time. Mari's mother is encouraging the same routine at home.

Within a few weeks, Hannah notices that Mari's nappy is dry for long periods of time and that Mari indicates when she needs to use the potty.

Summary

Forcing a child who is not ready to be toilet trained can cause conflict and create a traumatic experience for the child and their parents. However, being toilet trained and independent in using the toilet is an important developmental milestone and can contribute significantly to a child's self-confidence and sense of wellbeing.

Reference

STEARNS, J., SCHMIEDER, C. & MILLAR, E. (2011) *Level 3 Diploma for the Children and Young People's Workforce: Early Learning and Childcare.* London: HarperCollins Publishers.

Transitions

The term 'transitions' refers to changes during a child's day or life, for example during the routine of the day or when moving from pre-school to school. Change is a part of life for all children. As they grow and develop, their bodies change, their friendships and relationships change and they experience different situations involving transitions. Early years practitioners should deal sensitively with children who are experiencing transitions and provide support if necessary.

Most children experience some periods of transition during their life. These include not only physical transitions, such as starting school or moving house, but also physiological transitions, such as puberty, and emotional transitions, such as parents divorcing. Some children may also experience more extreme transitions, such as bereavement, moving to another country or going into foster care.

The effect of transitions on children's development

Children respond to transitions in different ways, both positively and negatively. Transition can affect all aspects of development and behaviour, but in most cases, the effects are short-lived.

Some of the negative effects of transitions on the development of children include:

➤ Regression: going back to the development or behaviour of a younger child, for example bed wetting or 'baby talk' (see *Regression*)

➤ Changes in behaviour: this can include becoming withdrawn or clingy, but also aggressive or attention-seeking behaviour (see *Challenging behaviour*)

➤ Physical problems: for example, food refusal, sleep disturbances and nightmares

➤ Speech problems: for example, stuttering or selective mutism (choosing not to speak)

➤ Mental problems: for example, lack of concentration or depression.

Supporting transitions

Change can be unsettling and can cause children to feel anxious and insecure. When children are experiencing change in their lives, they need consistent support. Sensitive adults should:

➤ provide stability and security, with consistent routines and predictable schedules

➤ offer information by explaining what is going to happen, using simple language

➤ listen, allowing time for information to be taken in and for children to respond

➤ be honest and truthful with children, especially when answering their questions, even if this is difficult

➤ acknowledge children's feelings, giving them the opportunity to express negative feelings, such as frustration or anger, and not dismissing or ignoring them (see *Resilience*)

➤ provide opportunities for play to help children explore different ideas and express their feelings, for example playing at doctors and nurses in preparation for going into hospital, or sharing a book about babies when a new baby is expected in the family. Expressive, creative and imaginative play, such as puppets, painting, small world play and stories, can help children to understand and come to terms with changes in their lives.

Case in point

Most children experience the transition of starting school or nursery and this can be an extremely stressful time for both parents and children. Research has shown that early years practitioners can support this process in different ways, including:

➤ Carrying out home visits to enable children and parents to meet early years staff in advance

➤ Encouraging frequent visits to the setting to provide familiarity for the child and parents

➤ Involving the parents fully in the transition process, sharing information and listening to their concerns

➤ Organising flexible, relaxed settling-in periods where parents can stay with their children and take their time in managing the separation

➤ Providing a predictable routine, which helps children to feel secure but is not too rigid

➤ Operating a key person system in the setting to provide each child with a strong attachment relationship with a practitioner who has a special responsibility for the child's welfare (see *Key person*).

Summary

During times of change and uncertainty, children need consistency and familiarity and they need to know that someone will continue to provide security for them. A strong attachment relationship with a trusted adult is important for children during times of transition. In early years settings, this is often their key person and it is the key person's responsibility to provide support, reassurance and stability at these times.

References

STEARNS, J., SCHMIEDER, C. & MILLAR, E. (2011) *Level 3 Diploma for the Children and Young People's Workforce: Early Learning and Childcare.* London: HarperCollins Publishers.

The Who Cares? Trust (supporting children in the care system) http://www.thewhocarestrust.org.uk

Winston's Wish (supporting children coping with bereavement) http://www.winstonswish.org.uk

Types of play

There are many different types of play, which have been categorised in a variety of ways. In his book *A Playworker's Taxonomy of Play Types*, Bob Hughes outlines 16 different types of play, although many share the same characteristics and overlap with each other. In early years, it is useful to classify five different types of play: physical, imaginative, creative, sensory and construction.

Physical play

Physical play is characterised by activities that use large and small physical movements. It incorporates 'rough and tumble' play and includes physical contact, strength and flexibility. Children can use lots of energy through jumping, climbing, chasing and balancing, and their play may involve equipment or apparatus, for example pedalling bikes, riding scooters, skipping and parachute games.

Physical play helps children to develop motor skills, body coordination, muscle strength, stamina and confidence and learn how to take risks safely. It provides opportunities for children to exercise their bodies and can therefore contribute towards preventing obesity and developing a healthy lifestyle (see *Outdoor learning*).

Imaginative play

Imaginative play is characterised by the make-believe world of children and 'let's pretend'. It incorporates fantasy and dramatic play and is often supported by 'props' such as dressing-up clothes or pretend food. Children may pretend to be another person or act out situations, taking on a variety of different roles, for example dressing up as a super hero, playing at being 'Mummy and Daddy' or pretending to be a dragon or a wizard.

Imaginative play helps children to develop their language and communication skills and their self-identity. It provides opportunities for children to express and manage their feelings, particularly when they are experiencing difficult situations, for example dealing with parental divorce or a new baby in the family (see *Transitions*).

Creative play

Creative play is characterised by self-expression. It involves the enjoyment of creation with a range of materials and tools, without the need for an end result. Children can design, explore, try out new ideas and make discoveries, with an element of surprise! It incorporates both exploratory and messy play, for example painting, sculpting, dancing, making music, digging and playing with sand, mud, water, clay and dough.

Creative play helps children to develop their curiosity and imagination and provides opportunities for children to express their thoughts and feelings and represent their ideas. This can be a valuable outlet for children who have difficulty with verbal expression, including children whose first language is not English (see *Communication*).

Sensory play

Sensory play is characterised by the exploration of materials using one or more of the five senses. Research has shown that early sensory experience fulfils an important function in infant brain development and the formation of neural pathways. This includes close, physical contact, soothing sounds and visual stimulation. Babies also benefit from sensory play opportunities, such as treasure baskets.

Sensory play for older children includes wet and dry sand, water, textured fabric, clay, dough and even foodstuffs, such as pasta or jelly. Outdoors, children can explore different sights, sounds, smells and textures in a sensory garden (see *Play resources*).

Construction play

Construction play is characterised by the building of three-dimensional objects using different materials, such as wood, card, plastic or recycled objects. It may also involve specifically manufactured toys. Construction play incorporates mastery and exploratory play, including manipulative behaviours, for example handling, throwing, banging or engaging with objects, such as stacking bricks.

Construction play helps children to develop spatial (space) awareness and hand–eye coordination. It also supports the development of problem-solving skills and an interest in how things work (see *Creative, critical thinking*).

Case in point

The staff team at Scallywags Nursery provide resources for a variety of different types of play, both inside and outside of the setting. Outdoors, the nursery has a wide variety of wheeled toys as well as a large garden where the children enjoy active games and can dig in the soil using their physical skills. The children have recently enjoyed the book *We're Going on a Bear Hunt* (Michael Rosen) and have been re-enacting parts of the story outside, making a 'cave' and using dressing-up clothes in their imaginative play. The outdoors has an area for sand and water as well as resources for painting and large-scale sculpture, where the children can engage in creative and constructive play.

Indoors, the practitioners provide a range of activities such as cutting with scissors, and threading beads, for the children to develop their fine motor physical skills. There is a well-equipped role-play area for imaginative play, which the practitioners change on a regular basis to follow the children's interests. Practitioners organise singing, dancing and music-making sessions with different instruments to encourage the children to express themselves in creative play. The children have been making pizza and enjoying the sensory experiences of mixing the dough, preparing the toppings and eating the finished products!

Summary

Early years practitioners should facilitate a wide variety of different types of play to stimulate children's all-round development and learning. Children will naturally engage in different types of play if they are given the opportunity and resources to do so.

References

HUGHES, B. (2002) *A Playworker's Taxonomy of Play Types.* 2nd Ed. London: PlayLink.

STEARNS, J., SCHMIEDER, C. & YOUNG, K. (2013) *BTEC National Children's Play, Learning and Development.* London: HarperCollins Publishers.

Vulnerable children

The National Children's Bureau (NCB) defines vulnerable children as those who are in need or who are most at risk of experiencing inequalities and poor life chances (NCB, 2013). Children may be considered vulnerable for a wide variety of reasons. Some children may experience physical problems, while others may live in situations that make them emotionally vulnerable.

Children in need

A child in need is one who is unlikely to reach or maintain a satisfactory level of health or development without the provision of support services. This includes disabled children as well as children whose health or development is likely to be significantly impaired (see *SEN*).

Children at risk

Some children are considered to be vulnerable because they are at risk of significant harm, for example through abuse or neglect. The statutory guidance in the government document *Working Together to Safeguard Children* (DfE, 2013) clearly outlines the roles of all professionals working to support children at risk. It also justifies compulsory intervention in family life to promote children's welfare (see *Safeguarding*).

Supporting vulnerable children

Vulnerable children have the same needs as all children (see *Basic needs of children*). They also have a number of special needs:

➤ Many vulnerable children experience a degree of insecurity in their lives for a variety of reasons, including traumatic family disruption, domestic violence or parental drug misuse. These children tend to live in the 'here and now' and need familiarity, routine and consistent boundaries to help them develop security and a sense of belonging.

➤ Many vulnerable children experience under-nurturing as a result of neglect, attachment disorders or abuse. They need warm, physical touch and nurturing relationships with significant adults to help them develop trust and resilience (see *Key person*).

➤ Vulnerable children need opportunities to express their feelings. They often feel confused, angry, sad and frustrated, which they find difficult to understand. Creative play activities help children to express their feelings, for example small world play, painting or role-play (see *Resilience*).

Multi-agency working is very important in supporting vulnerable children. Different professionals work together using the Common Assessment Framework (CAF) to identify the needs of vulnerable children and their families and to determine how these needs can best be met (see *Multi-agency working*).

The National Children's Bureau (NCB) operates a Vulnerable Children Programme, which focuses on children whose experience of adverse factors in their lives makes them vulnerable to significant risk of reduced life chances. This could include poor educational achievement and reduced employment opportunities.

Case in point

Polly is three years old and lives with her mother, stepfather, two older brothers and a baby sister in bed and breakfast accommodation. Her stepfather is unemployed, and is currently on probation following a conviction for theft. Her mother has acute post-natal depression and struggles to keep the children adequately clothed and fed.

Polly attends Stepping Stones Nursery every day. She is frequently hungry, tired, inappropriately dressed, very withdrawn and reluctant to participate in any activities.

Polly would be considered vulnerable because she is a child at risk and in need of services. Without appropriate intervention, Polly's health and development will be significantly impaired and this will have an impact on her life chances.

Summary

Life can be extremely challenging for vulnerable children. They are often affected by domestic violence, poverty and low self-esteem. Neglect, abuse and isolation can make their home life unbearable. Multi-agency working is extremely important in supporting vulnerable children and helping them to reach their full potential.

References

Department for Education (2013) *Working Together to Safeguard Children: A Guide to Inter-agency Working to Safeguard and Promote the Welfare of Children.* http://www.education.gov.uk

National Children's Bureau http://www.ncb.org.uk

The Children's Society http://www.childrenssociety.org.uk

Index

Index

Index